DARK PSYCHOLOGY

Learn How to Analyze People with the Secrets of Manipulation, Mind Control and NLP

by Franz Harper

© **Copyright 2020 by Franz Harper**

All rights reserved.

This document is geared towards providing exact and reliable information with regards to the topic and issue covered. The publication is sold with the idea that the publisher is not required to render accounting, officially permitted, or otherwise, qualified services. If advice is necessary, legal or professional, a practiced individual in the profession should be ordered.

- From a Declaration of Principles which was accepted and approved equally by a Committee of the American Bar Association and a Committee of Publishers and Associations.

In no way is it legal to reproduce, duplicate, or transmit any part of this document in either electronic means or in printed format. Recording of this publication is strictly prohibited and any storage of this document is not allowed unless with written permission from the publisher. All rights reserved.

The information provided herein is stated to be truthful and consistent, in that any liability, in terms of inattention or otherwise, by any usage or abuse of any policies, processes, or directions contained within is the solitary and utter responsibility of the recipient reader. Under no circumstances will any legal responsibility or blame be held against the publisher for any reparation, damages, or monetary loss due to the information herein, either directly or indirectly.

Respective authors own all copyrights not held by the publisher.

The information herein is offered for informational purposes solely, and is universal as so. The presentation of the information is without contract or any type of guarantee assurance.

The trademarks that are used are without any consent, and the publication of the trademark is without permission or backing by the trademark owner. All trademarks and brands within this book are for clarifying purposes only and are the owned by the owners themselves, not affiliated with this document.

Table Of Contents

Introduction 1

Chapter One 6

The Dark Side Psychology Of The Insane 6

The Psychology Of Color 23

The Deeper Black Meaning 29

How To Make People Like You Instantly? 34

How To Overcome Your Psychological? 40

Meeting Our Dark Side Benefits 49

Chapter Two 52

Dark Psychological Techniques To Get Your Ex Back 52

How To Influence People With The Subconscious Mind? .. 54

Where Is Your Mind And Your Heart? 56

How To Win Influence People And Friends? 73

Influence People At Work 76

The Benefit Of Npl 83

Chapter Three 86

How To Influence People To Reach Their Full Potential? ... 86

Persuasive Methods To Influence People 93

Exploring Mind Control History And Programming 116

Twelve Strategies Ways To Win Friends And Influence People 128

Knowing The Woman's Mind 134
Freedom Of The Soul And Mind Intelligence 142
Conclusion 148

INTRODUCTION

As people say, knowledge is power. Well, if the experience is power, the equivalent of having a superpower is knowledge of human psychology. Psychology, the perception of the human mind, and the way it operates are a central theme of human existence. From advertising, religion, crime, finance, and love for hate, psychology underpins everything. Someone who understands psychological principles holds the key to human influence.

It is often a difficult task to acquire psychological knowledge. Like every advanced secret of the human race, subjective experience is deeply buried in the pages of obscure journals and held outside the public's grasp. To distill this powerful knowledge in a useful way, someone would have to search through countless books and newspapers, trying to separate what are helpful from what is useless.

Dark psychology in the world is at work. Perhaps you don't like this, so you can't change it. So there's a choice: either try to ignore something substantial and risk getting your next victim, or take control of your situation and learn to defend yourself and loved ones from people who would destroy you by their constant psychological manipulation.

Dark psychology is not just a defensive measure. In the field of dark psychology, ideas, and principles will help you to make progress in your personal and professional endeavors. Nobody asks you to become a psychopath, but you can definitely use a little more energy in your everyday life.

Dark psychology is the art of manipulation and control of the mind. While psychology is the study of human actions and the center of our thought, movement, and communication, it is dark psychology that uses motivating, manipulative, convincing, and coercive strategies to get what they want.

- Machiavellianism: Manipulation is used to mislead, manipulate and have no moral sense.

- Narcissism: selfishness, superiority and compassion.

- Psychopathy: Often charming and friendly but with impulsivity, egotism, lack of empathy, and remorselessness.

None of us want to be a deceptive target, but it happens quite often. We may not be exposed to someone in the Dark Triad, but every day, ordinary people face daily dark psychological tactics.

Such strategies are often used in marketing, internet advertising, sales, and even the actions of our boss. If you have children (particularly young people), then you will most certainly experience such strategies as your children play with behaviors to get what they want and try independence. Yes, subtle deception and dark intimidation are often used by people you have faith and love. Here are some of the techniques most widely used by ordinary people.

Love Flooding–Compliments, love or buttering someone to ask Lie–distortion, mistruth, partial truths, misleading stories Love Denial–No attention and affection Retirement–No people or silent treatment–Choose constraints–Offer other options which divert you from the possibility that someone does not want to make reverse psychology–tell a person one–

Semantic Manipulation–The manipulator tells you that he or she has a different definition and interpretation of the conversation with terms that are believed to have similar or shared meanings.

It shows us all how easy it is to use these tactics to achieve what we want. Evaluate your strategies in every area of your life, love, management, including job, parent ship, and friendship.

While some people using these dark strategies know precisely what they do and want to trick you into getting what they want, others use dark and deceptive techniques without understanding it entirely. Many of these people learned strategies from their parents during their youth. Others practiced strategies during their childhood or in their adulthood. They unintentionally used a manipulation tactic, and it worked. They have what they wanted, what they needed. Consequently, strategies continue to help them get their way.

In some situations, these techniques are educated. Training programs that teach grim, deceptive psychological, and methods of persuasion usually are sales or advertising. Many of these services use dark strategies to create a brand or to sell a product purely to support themselves or their company, not their customers. Many of these training programs convince people that using these tactics are all right and for the buyer's benefit. And their lives are, of course, much happier when they buy the product or service.

CHAPTER ONE

The Dark Side Psychology of the Insane

Psychology has tried to raise human souls in recent years by using many common psychological concepts such as "Positive Psychology" or the many books that have been written to tell people how to conduct their successful lives from talking about parachutes, ten steps towards something, mired with titles how to and much more. Most of them are just misplaced pop psychology or fad of the moment. Can life be as easy as reading the right book and following certain basic concepts, and all will be fine for you and me? This paper is special, and we are going to explore the Dark Side of the human mind— the part that sees disengagement, devastation, vile acts as part of the human psyche which comes up within us every time — the part which finds excitation, joy, and enjoyment in the dysfunctional part of our life. How could society reconcile itself with its dark side? The term foolish applies to those who disregard social norms in society.

Let's first examine how the "dark side" of psychological thought and behavior can be identified. To know what is normal and what is considered an unusual behavior, we need a scale. Our first indicator is social norms, which in any culture means that ordinary activity is deemed to be reasonable in the situations in which our expectations are challenged. In western culture, for instance, striking another person violently is considered a criminal act and a repulsive act against a peaceful society.

Nonetheless, we endorse violence when the person receives social permission, such as the soldier in the war, a policeman in the arrest of a dangerous criminal, a citizen who protects his family from another person's serious threat. These double standards can, in many ways, be misunderstood. The soldier who commits war crimes such as genocide, the police officer who uses violence to intimidate a witness when questioning them or the individual who violates the rights of another person to benefit his or her role.

The second is a reliable measure? How do we decide what is right and wrong as a society, who has the power to determine such rights, whether laws comply with moral convictions or whether they are the poor shielded from the powerful or from the rich? All societies agree that killing another human being runs counter to moral law—killing is just wrong, and the community that supports its law-makers in their honest, legal position should be punished by an act of equal severity.

For most societies, this was an ethical code of conduct, such as 10 Christian commandments and others, from Buddhism to the Muslim Koran. Faith in divine reward and punishment is expressed in the legal language and laws that constitute the foundation of any civilized nation. Once these rules have been adopted, then why do we deviate readily from these social, law, and religious guidelines that allow us to live in a peaceful society governed by agreed codes of behavior that protect people from risk, injury, and abuse?

The third area of action is that it does not lay down the law or moral principles but the everyday activities that the English call "manners" or "political." The action or manner of acting that conforms to the conduct recognized as that of the highest member of a society who is capable of acting in the company of others according to a number of standards that are seen as marking advanced civilization.

This can sometimes be seen in table manner etiquette or in a man who opens the door to a woman and enables them first to acknowledge the human duty to protect and protect women. Women's rights in certain cultures today have cast doubt on women's ways as sexists and therefore degrading to women's independence. Never without etiquette is seen to be a characteristic of a well-broad culture, whether it be formal English or a Japanese tea ceremony.

After establishing different societies for measuring behavior, law, morals, or socially acceptable standards human beings are still behaving in a wide variety of dysfunctions which often affect and influence other individuals to the point where they do not see the law, moral codes and the etiquette of the rest of society. Sometimes by the sense of guilt, we all know when we have transgressed specific rules that for a well-ordered society, we see as necessary. However, there are others who feel nothing about coping with destruction, violence, and death as merely their right to live without these laws and the freedom to live a life that is defined only by what they want to own, own, or kill.

The Dark-Side: what the guy who kicks the dog possesses if he's irritated by a society that thinks about his life. What are the thoughts when the dog screams and howls in agony and fright? Why does he smile and wish the dog more harm and genuinely enjoy the sight of an animal? The spectator is appalled by his actions and sympathy to the defenseless dog for which this man has received inhuman, unrepentant treatment. Who is this man? Who is this man? Why he's all of us sometimes. We all lose our sense of emotional calmness and reason as we struggle with unfairness or lack of opportunity.

On the other side, wait for the rich man to have accomplished everything he wanted, but he is still delighted to kick and watch the dog suffer from his paws. A sense of superiority in his ability to inflict pain and a satisfaction in feeling superior to other smaller people that he sees as unable to take what they want. This excellent situational mindset leads to a lack of sympathy or empathy for others as follies who take over their hegemony as leaders and legislators.

The example above also gives an insight into a behavior that violates our three definitions of social laws, the law (hurting a defenseless animal) morally acceptable in social terms (tabuing senseless actions viewed as wrong) (whereas everyone the lose their temper and kick a dog, most people will feel tribulation and sorrow). But here we meet people who feel no shame, no regret and see themselves as excluded from the laws with which they disagree. Fox hunting in England was mostly a cruel sport done by educated, skilled, wealthy men and women? Yet these same people claimed that they had a right to hunt and destroy a defenseless animal for a while as their hounds grabbed and devoured a mouse. Although the majority of English people voted to prohibit this sport on some occasions, it took several years for it to become law.

Today fox-hunting is an illegal activity, but the same people continue to violate the law and to hunt under local legislation, which still has to comply with national legislation. We know what they are doing is illegal, unethical, and contrary to social standards, as described by majority opinion. Nevertheless, they say that they are more excellent parts of society and thus ethical obligations for ordinary masses on a daily basis.

In England, these people are parliamentarians, police, judges, and others who are governing aspects of society in England, such as landlords (a property sometimes granted stealing the legitimate land of poor people by the Royal consent of the past). In other words, those who would set an example for society are the same people who flaunt the law and have socially acceptable behavior.

We have to look at the suspect in another case. Criminals are often seen as society's rejects because they come from dysfunctional backgrounds, deprived communities, and inadequate parental education. Yet the most significant damage to the public of society is often caused by corporate crime, including the mix-up of pension funds, the selling of stocks and shares, corruption of property and resources by CEOs and government officials.

This so-called white-collar crime is often undetected and the most difficult to prosecute. Every day offenders are more visible to the public, as their actions cause community uproar and make the press scream for action by the police and civil authorities. Thus most laws deal with visual violence, which is easy to understand and understand.

The prosecution for visual abuse in our courts and press is also straightforward. How can we differentiate between the two types of criminals-the so-called violence of victims of white-collar criminals who do not see a direct casualty or the killer who murders and kills those who resist their will to steal from society and the suffering they leave behind?

Then what has psychology to say about the deviants who do not regard their acts as an annoyance to themselves and feel that others are not vulnerable in their lives and thus deserve to be victims of those who are smarter, stronger, or more powerful?

The press is often shouting over passive masses who accept the status quo, and would the local person who took the law into their own hands maybe condemn them or their families to take revenge on wrongdoings?

The first place where psychology reveals the causes behind others ' dark actions is "developmental" that learning is along this path that the dog kicker has not been adequately treated and taken care of. They were subjected to cruelty, sexual abuse, or lack of social education during their formative years. The same transgressors are targeted by bullying at school, which means that those who are vulnerable in society must be disappointed with themselves.

The question we have to ask here is why some of the perpetrators are probably most law-abiding and are only a handful that become the monsters that murder and mutilate for evolutionary errors? Most scientists at this stage like to point to a genetic comportment element. For some time now, this old chestnut has been around.

In violent criminals, there is evidence that they often have an extra Y chromosome (men), which gives them high testosterone levels, which lead to violence in stressful circumstances in which anxiety and fear are the answer to what they need. Nevertheless, this is statistically minute as a proportion of violent criminals, although it may be higher in the general population of jails.

All genetic research to date has led to genetic factors being hypothesized but no concrete evidence to support the allegations. The most important finding is that twin studies in which twins are separated at birth have a high incidence of similar behavior and outcomes. Again as a proportion of twins that have been born and tested, this evidence is low for genetic determinism and reliable for developmental environments, and twins have backgrounds that are so stable that if they have been different, it is more likely to be a surprise. So, if we exclude developmental results, genetic predispositions, what makes some people socially acceptable and some people who meet all of society's requirements? This is the type of proposition that makes psychology difficult to always see as a positive view or a deterministic world direction and that perhaps it is reasonable conduct in humans that, on several occasions, is cruel, manipulative, abusive, and criminal. Such morals are the luxury of a settled society in which everyone is economically and in caste or class.

The Survivalist Psychology: There are primarily those in the United States that see society's end as a real chance, whether they support nuclear annihilation (now more likely bio-war) or the break-up of capitalism that leads to social mess and civil strife. Such individuals are often called victims.

We store arms against the uncontrollable mobs that would overrun the country in case of a civil disintegration, and food for the risk of economic meltdown shortages. (In 2009 most victims in the United States would argue that they have a good case). Survivors claim that they have a constitutional right to defend themselves and their families in the event of a societal collapse and lack of security legislation. Occasionally, these organizations disagree with existing laws imposed by federal authorities such as the FBI.

Therefore, the attitude of the survivor is seen as a sincere attempt to control its own fate against potential disasters while, on the one hand, it is in conflict with society and on the other side. After all, insurance undertakings only thrive under this assumption and would be perhaps the first one not to survive an economic collapse in capitalism, as seen by many bank's failures in 2008/2009 worldwide.

The most popular movies today at the box office are disaster films that cause the societal destruction of society with the flood, sun flares, nuclear warfare, alien invasions, and other disasters. The protagonists of these films are always resourceful survivors who protect their children from all threats using violence. Why do people find these people admirable, as victims, but the actual perpetrators, as public foes of the status quo, are vilified? Judging from the popularity of these movies, ordinary people understand that the breakdown of society may happen or is inevitable.

And they interpret these films as a kind of hope for another future, which can emerge from the collapse of their daily life.

The psychology of evolution: all people started in human history as survivors as hunter collectors who roamed the land in search of easily accessible animals for food and warmth. Over time, we see these communities settling down in agro-cultural settlements establishing rules, regulations, leaders, and a moral code. As these existing cultures develop and grow, they create art, music, and religion to offset a restricted life within the constraints of their learning. Land and property become critical from these beginnings. The possession of goods and chattels is essential for production.

Over time, these settlements become villages, towns, and cities, which ultimately form borders. Survival now becomes the team, not the entity, as human instincts have been since the beginning of time.

But all these systems eventually disappear and crumble. Some for unknown reasons like the Mayan and other cultures in South America. Many struggle as they become kingdoms, which with a version of their laws and religions, rule the poor.

But one thing history teaches us all is that for all sorts of reasons societies disappear. (Greek, Romanesque, Ancient World Egyptian and Modern World British, French, German and Japanese empires).

All these cultures have one thing in common that they had not foreseen their destruction. A European and American in the present world could not imagine the collapse of the EEC or the United States, but these new modern powers have their own triumphant Achilles, "Capitalism." Although Karl Marx had seen the drawbacks and eventual failure of capitalism, he could not have seen how it engulfed the modern world to such a point that oil and gas wars were going to rule the 21st century.

Nevertheless, Marx would probably laugh gleefully at the collapse of the banking system in 2009 based on greed and debt among the world's first nations. Most of the failures may lead to mismanagement, but it was a loss of confidence by average people in the financial system that caused the money rushed and debt crushed by high-interest rates and poor returns on investment. If people panic, they reach survival mode-they first take care of themselves.

It is time to conclude at this point from this experience that social norms, rules, and values are indeed "natural" for people and that society always imposes collective actions based on what influential people want over the powerless.

This mentality of survival is indeed our norm and what society seeks to do is to control the wild beast in every human being by training them from an early age to obey the laws, regulations, and morals of the controlling body, usually of the rich who control our governments and institutions.

Therefore, must we denounce those who feel that society does not give them a fair deal-what should they do in reality to survive in an often hostile environment in which privileges rely on your education, family or wealth? Should psychology itself have to leave the closet and accept that reasonable human conduct is against traditional cultures and rules? The people resent society, in reality, but they experience some helplessness in trying to live with the sheep because they are powerless against those who regulate legislation and morality. Is it any wonder, then, that sometimes a single individual takes it into its hands to change society or its climate, to live a free and self-controlled life away from the rigors of cultures, which we all saw crumble and reinvent themselves once again when the newly wealthy and powerful take control?

In the last century, we saw China go from a depot-dominated empire to a military rule ruled by the rich and powerful, to become a communist stare of the 1950s, where Marxism determined a fair life for everyone and eventually a capitalist, socialist state founded on a ruling party that established the lives of the powerless population which, indeed, was fighting for. Will another revolution happen in China in the future–currently, given the unrest of minorities forced to comply with the central rule in many parts of China, seems unlikely?

Unable to see their downfall, all empires! How then will psychology deal with this issue of human behavior as an underlying survival mechanism whereby human beings inevitably become aggressive, cruel, and dominant among weaker people?

In mental hospitals, psychiatric is often seen as an agent in social control, so you have to be committed and controlled for the safety and benefit of all if you do not agree with society and its rules.

Psychology, on the other hand, is considered to be the liberating aspect of mental health when we help those who are not in tune with society to find their place and fit into what is deemed to be standard for this group. What is the answer for those who rebel against the community in which they live and want to live another way of life by the interference of the powerful and the freedom to live a life they choose as appropriate? Or do we wait–before films come into force–for the tragedy awaiting all people and the return to the dog-eat-dog life called survival–the real social standard!

The Psychology of Color

The study of color psychology as a result of human emotions and cognition Psychology of color is mostly still in the domain of folk or popular psychology and is commonly connected to culture. Although there are no experimental color studies or a scientifically valid' color theory,' color meaning may easily be attributed to specific perceptions, emotions, and circumstances. The color psychology explores the color effects on human emotions and behavior. Red usually makes people fervent or happy and white is pure and clean, yellow raises alertness, loss, black a sense of mystery, and anonymity.

Some of earlier color theories and their relationship with psychology can be found back to Goethe, who argues that colors can have and adhere to spiritual relations to produce extreme emotional situations such as blue and red generate emotional states. The possibility of associating individual characteristics traits with color preferences. Nevertheless, these studies have long been considered unscientific and misleading, and no general scientific consensus on the color effects on human emotions has been reached. However, color theory and the alleged impact of colors have been widely acknowledged and applied throughout life, from publicity to interior design.

Colors standard in nature, such as green, black, and brown, are more appropriate, while blue tends to have a sooting protective effect as the color of the sky or the water bodies and people equate blue with harmony, tranquility, and serenity. Green is the color of the leaves and symbolizes the new life, personal development, and improvement. Brown is a neutral color that still stands for earthiness, texture, and wholesomeness.

Natural color, simply because of their familiarity, is well received and universal, which can be used in pigments for advertisements or products. Natural products should be sold in natural colored boxes or bottles or reflect the product color. Lemon juice is best served in a colored bottle, yellow or green, rather than orange. In reality, red bottles with blue labels for mineral water are paired with cocoa in the case of advertisements and services; and such already defined brand associations should be considered prior to launch goods and commercials. An utterly black drink can be regarded as mysterious, harmful, or even toxic, and also, if the substance inside is pretty harmless, sales are affected. In fact, brown else a combination of brown and black could be better for fizzy drinks or coffee or cocoa than the black only as the containers of the color. Containers or bottles in neutral colors such as light brown, beige, aged golden would be more appropriate for selling beer or soda.

Likewise, websites should also improve the spirit and fashionable colors of products or services provided. A wedding site should be white or rose as its primary color, and a funeral site might be black or grips as its primary color. However, this is culturally different as events like birth, death, and marriage are represented in different societies in different colors. Red represents celebration and marriage in some East cultures, while white is commonly used in marriage in Western societies. White is used in Eastern cultures as a color of death, sterility, and destruction, whilst in the West; black is a color of lamentation and loss. The use of colors in different cultures and societies may provide insights into cultural concepts, as white representing death in eastern nations signifies not only high levels of purity but also rebirth and a change of shape. The fact that death is widely believed in the East can also be considered a cause for celebration rather than mourning. Therefore, generally speaking, all events can be viewed as frequently depicted with white. Death in the west is synonymous with death, evil, end or loss, and black, as the notion of regeneration is not present in western societies for the next stage of life. This may be the central difference between materialistic and spiritualistic cultures, which also provides insights into color psychology.

Psychology will have to explore the effect of colors on humans more thoroughly and objectively in the use of colors in practical life. There are certain color studies related to vision and perception, although the main mechanisms of color perception are: attention-as measured in reaction time when a color association is seen-as measured with a preference for a specific color to reflect particular events and circumstances. We are quickly drawn to yellow, red, and orange, though the association of particular colors with specific events can contribute to a general preference for such colors. While red is generally preferred as an emergency color for emergencies or warnings and does not create a similar correlation with ambulance or fire service and any other color. White is high but may not be visible or noticeable during the day. Therefore, color perception depends not only on the attention given to color properties but also on color association with specific characteristics based on our social or cultural awareness. It can, in some way, invoke human emotions, although another kind of research is needed for the emotional aspect of color psychology. Retention is the last stage of color perception, which in effect evokes reactions as in our memory, we expect those colors have associative values and characteristics, and so on, blue means calm, red means love, white means purity and peace and so on.

Therefore, color psychology should have two different branches-

- Color effects on human emotions–psychological and social elements of color psychology that cause human emotions
- Color effects on human understanding and perception–the physiological color reactions, and biological, including stages of treatment, interaction, retention.

In psychology, these color effects must be incorporated to understand the real sense of color when influencing human reactions, feelings, emotions, and behaviors. Such two distinct branches of color psychology should not only be included as a theoretical framework in the study of color psychology but as a functional framework to use color psychology in advertising, products, and services. We live in times of great significance for the visual media with ads for goods and advertisements on the internet, television, magazines, posters, etc. Visual stimuli are a significant aspect of modern life, as visual information assaults us, and color's function tends to be essential to our visual experiences.

Color Psychology should, therefore, be researched and applied in a systematic and empirical way, to every aspect of human undertakings including businesses and education, and it will have to be studied as a holistic organization to understand the mental, social, physical, political, and emotional aspects of psychology.

The Deeper Black Meaning

Black isn't such a light. Black is white, and black is almost blank. It absorbs light and reflects nothing. So it is warmer than white that reflects all colors but does not retain any. While both black and white are not shades, they are responsible, as symbols of lightness and darkness, for all our beautiful hues.

Black is related to total darkness and the unknown emotionally. It's contrary to white. Whereas black is frequently associated with evil, white is light, pure, and useful. Both have positive and negative aspects. White stands for daylight. The light not only warms and enlightens the soul but can lead to blindness when light rays are too intense. On the other hand, darkness makes all invisible and therefore causes fear. Yet it is the darkness in meditation that allows us to relax and focus, to discover the inner truth, the internal light.

Black and white is inseparable, in fact. We form an absolute polarity as symbols of light and darkness. When the sun is extinguished, silence occurs, and darkness disappears when there is light.

Like every color, black has two characteristics that are very contrasting. The negative side is a shame, sadness, heaviness, and, at its peak, darkness. This reflects stability, width, concentration, strength, weight, and exclusivity positively. It is enigmatic and profoundly profound. Those who don't fear it will experience it as being highly spiritual in black; those who fear it will regard it as dangerous and evil.

Black is used to describing the terrifying and mysterious. This stands for exclusivity, like the black limo or the black nightdress. It definitely represents the favorite hue for luxury and prestige. The immense depth gives it a strong attraction.

Why is psychological awareness of danger triggering organism response? PSYCHOLOGY OF FEAR The reason is in the case of human anatomy, more specifically because of discomfort. Should psychological pain imitate physical pain?

How does suffering happen? Everything is very evident with physical pain. They do not take simple motor reflexes under the command of the spinal cord into account.

During the sensation of the physical receptor, the nervous impulses are transmitted through nerves to the individual part of the brain. A sense of discomfort exists.

How does psychological pain happen? The role of our organism is to self-regulate all physiologic processes, that is to say, brain responses to changes in organism chemical processes.

It is possible that some changes occur under the influence of emotions in the body, such as blood concentration, and then it is transmitted to the brain, and the stimulation of brain responses is transmitted to one of the organs, and pain occurs. May it name the pain's emotional source.

Now we should understand how emotions affect the organism's physical condition. The complex structure of the nervous system and mentality must be followed. For this reason, a specialist is required.

For example, when you are afraid of darkness, you have heartburn, floridity, and throat discomfort. You sound like someone's stopping your escape. Here you're not scared darkness itself, but of something in the shadow. It is based on the information you got during your lifetime. You fear something the devil may do with you. You fear. A young child never fears darkness until it has been shown what could be there. Let it actively call terror.

Phobias such as fear of a specific situation or event, which frighten you with something and increase the feeling of anxiety and panic, often, relate to conscious fear as a result of your bad experience or the negative information obtained from someone. What is this fear's nature? How is this terror happening? What do I feel? What do I think? Lack of trust, Dejection, Pressure, Awkwardness, Inactivity, Blame, Death, Injury, The dismay, Depression, Stress, Anxiety, Panic. You have trouble feeling in your rose. Wind difficulty. Air difficulty. Cold sweat. Hot sweat. These are the body's psychological and physical sensations. And that means that fear is related to other negative emotions. One aspect affects the other, it comes from the other, but it means the same.

What about subconscious apprehension or not based on experience, in other words? What can it be?

This can be the fear of uncertainty, the fear of the unknown. Kids, for example, the alarm sounds unknown things. Basically, people were always terrified of unexplained acts of nature from the very beginning of human history. Or was their fear based on a previous phenomenon?

For example, fear of an unknown future, fear of possible negative fantasies. How can we learn that these are terrible events? We equate incidents with adverse events we have witnessed.

It turns out that we hate new things because we dislike unknown things. We're not afraid of hidden positive things because they awaken joy. And when we're so scared, we forget all the right events. In other words, when a mistaken image is created in our minds about an unknown occasion, a sense of fear arises from negative, early-experienced fear. This means the fear of something strange is a conscious fear.

How to Make People like You Instantly?

Both people like it, and yet a lot of people go through life, or at least part of their lives, feeling like people don't like it. This chapter aims to start talking about what you can do to feel and like–maybe' instantly.' Many people judge someone within the first 30 seconds of meeting them for the first time. You must, therefore, realize that the way you first meet someone in the most successful and' like' approach.

In reality, when you talk to someone, they usually' instantly dimensioned you' and begin to' take the mind' to determine if you are probably a person to whom they could connect as soon as they see you.

This means that you have to' feel' like an attractive friend-and that doesn't mean you have to look' film star' or cat-walk! What it does mean, however, is that you have to see your appearance transparent, polite, frank, outgoing, and' as if you matter.'

Cleanliness is next to godliness' was often said. It is the case when making an immediate impression that a decision should be taken as to whether your garments look at least clean and well looked after. Your hair, teeth, skin, and other visible external indicators are' good.' So, always make sure your appearance has been taken into account no matter how well you communicate-if you proceed to smile and expose the slice of spinach on your teeth, this will ruin your chances!

You must also realize that you don't seem to be wrapped in yourself, or somehow disturbed. It is essential that you demonstrate your interest in a new person. This can mean physical contact in a supportive and comfortable way. Maybe this means shaking your hands or even greeting people in a somewhat' intimate' way. But you must be sure of yourself to begin communicating probability in the right direction.

When you are introduced, it is imperative to have clear eye-to-eye contact with someone-which means looking at them directly in their eyes-with a warm and sincere smile. If you lack confidence and are typically not a' smiley' person, you need to make some serious effort in this area-while making sure that you don't give an idea of deception or' overdo it,' which is likely to have the opposite effect to your intention.

Once you start talking, the next' big thing' that will influence people is. You must give your voice a vibrant and friendly tone. Unfortunately, some people develop their sound to a monotonous or dull tone. Or perhaps they are talking in a squeaky or affected manner. You need to be auto critical in this matter, and if you find that you are missing, you need to make an effort to improve the skills of speech. It can be done-actors and actresses make it live, and when you become comfortable in yourself and the way you sound, many of the other' like' qualities will be created.

When you managed to give a new person the right first visual and audible experience, then you are already ready to be' instantly friendly.' The rest will focus on how you talk first. The key is to remember that people "like" to be asked about themselves, their lives, their likes and dislikes–in other words, and they feel like they are your focus. Customers don't want to hear the stories of the "Awesome I am" or to monopolize the conversation so that they can't get a word in. If you can manage it well, say about 60 to 40 percent in your favor (or even 71:31), when it comes to who talks the best, this will make you' instantly fun' as a' good listener' is most people.

Nevertheless, if you meet someone who's the quiet and retired man, it can take some effort to get them accessible and relax. This means that you need the ability to ask "healthy appropriate" questions. You are asking what they like. What do they want? How do they feel about it? (Anything that seems appropriate)? What are they doing? And other gentle private questions that you can ask indicate that you are' genuinely' interested in them. You will be much more likable if you seem genuinely interested.

Also, make sure you are focused on the person you are living with — created a digital' bubble' of attention around you— including recognizing that for some reasons you may be uncomfortable and trying to handle it (this may vary from triggers such as' awkward' discussion topics to' hardware!').

Remember that at all times, you must keep your posture open and friendly. For example, when talking, folding your arms is a' no' because it creates a psychological barrier. But it's imperative "signs" to hold a focus on people as they speak and to demonstrate you are listening carefully with nodes and sounds of agreement, as necessary. It is generally suggested that the mirroring of the person with whom you communicate will help to build empathy and enhance the development of your relationship.

One of the most fabulous tips is to try to develop a natural, warm, and pleasant smile that you use freely. Individuals want' happy people' with whom they are enjoyable. On and on, both men and women are drawn to someone that can make them laugh (But do not get stressed out and you feel that you have to know the contents of a' funny book'—laughter needs to be reasonable and fun to work best!) At the end of the day you have to note-there is no point in pretending to be what you are not. Pretense will finally be revealed most often. You should be "natural," trustworthy, friendly, open-minded– and it may take time and practice to deal with the areas of your present behavior that do not fit your bill. So not only do you need to improve interpersonal skills from personal presentation to personal interaction as described but also the attributes that you create must be part of REAL you. If there's a feeling on people that you are' fake,' you won't succeed in gaining success.

Eventually-people will like you for what you are. If you like you don't want people instantly; it may not be that bad when you know they will like you for who you are. However, if you realize that you have some flaws in the way you relate to other people, you need to work on them in a determined way, because no pretense or rehearsal can guarantee that being' instantly friendly' lasts for you.

How to Overcome Your Psychological?

It is important to remember that at any point, you are not your complex and to differentiate your identity from your compound. Don't blame yourself because your system is only a collection of faulty assumptions formed by your brain.

You should be able to overcome your complexities and move closer to your desired being by following the steps below methodology. You will try to read through sentences, consider and follow the principle when going through the steps.

Trust motion only. Life exists at the level of actions, not words.'

I. REALITY The first step is to know and to appreciate the current complexes. I don't remember your complicated means to be kept in the dark, suffer, and fight something that you can't define. You need to look deep inside and identify the root of your complex's negative emotional behaviors. Monitor your emotional complex feelings and use them as a guide to learn more about the essence of your situation.

But don't try to suppress, judge, or reject these feelings, it will only make them grow and escalate. You must release them, observe them, and learn from them by finding the triggers behind them. You must first get to know your enemy before you kill him.

II.ACCEPTANCE The second step is to accept yourself and stop judging. Even for those parts, you want to improve before you begin your trip to conquer your complex, you must embrace yourself and value yourself for who you are now. This is a general concept, not only mental constructs. The biggest reason why most people don't embrace themselves is that they think it will inspire change and improve their lives. Yet recognition of yourself is a prerequisite for progress and for you to fulfill your true potential. Don't be afraid that you won't improve by acknowledging your current situation because adaptation is a part of human nature.

To gain acceptance of yourself, you must, first of all, recognize certain facets of yourself you do not like and understand that they have been built to defend against' threats' that you may have met earlier in your life. For example, if your parents have disciplined you for your poor school grades, you may have progressed towards academic success. You must also be mindful of and embrace these undesirable aspects of your life (e.g., intellect, appearance, food). You should realize that they feel and need to be fulfilled, e.g., with the feeling that you are not smart enough for low self-confidence emotions and that you can only satisfy them by doing your brain. Usually, you will have two opposing forces in your mind, one struggling to overcome and sustain (often subconsciously) these unforeseen aspects of your life. Your aim should be to strike the right balance between these two powers by a dialogue. Ultimately, note that your lives or structures are far more than these unwanted things.

III.FORGIVENESS The third step is to forgive yourself for suffering from this complex and to allow yourself free from the complex. You most likely wish that you never had to suffer from this challenge and that you were angry about all the negative emotions and behaviors that uncertainty causes in your lives. But it's not your fault; don't blame yourself for suffering from your complex.

Perhaps you were young when your complex was created, and you did not know anything better, you did not understand the internal process that led to your complexity. Perhaps you did not have the resources, the skills, and the power to combat it at that time. But the past is meaningless, now is the only moment. And since you have come so far, it means that you are ready and willing to free yourself. Forgive yourself what you have had to bear and be proud of yourself and happy that your old restricting patterns and feelings will free you now. Allow your mind's doors to open up to a new life of liberation as you approach your life's fulfillment and visions.

IV. DEEPEN AND EXPECT OF YOUR COMPLEX. Although you are de-motivated to write down stuff and challenge the efficacy of those strategies, note that writing is a proven resource of personal development since it helps you to place your thoughts on a new level. STEP 3 (the next two steps enable you to compose your ideas so that you can achieve the desired outcome)

Through completing the following activities, you hope to appreciate further and deepen your origins in several areas of your system. Please answer the following questions about your complex by examining your emotions:

• What feelings and thoughts accompany your psychological complex and which produce the highest emotional burden in you?

• Which are some of the common elements of the inner conversation you tend to have with your complex?

• Write down every thought you have about your complex in a sincere way for 10 minutes. Don't try to write in a structured manner, and it's all about freely sharing anything within your mind–you'd be shocked to see how many things you didn't know about.

• What do you consider to be the main obstacles and doubts that hinder you from solving your mental complex?

- How far are you prepared to go from 1 to10 to solve your complex? Why? Why?

- When you succeeded in solving your dilemma, how would your life be different?

- What are your beliefs about your mental system if it were not a concern for you? E.g., with regard to complicated money, it would be liberating to believe that money is easy to make, money is not happy, and money is not the center of your life.

Write the responses to the above questions. You should be able to identify different points but also resistances of your complex that you were not aware of before. Try to list the most important.

V. CREATE TO YOUR COMPLEX NEW PERSPECTIVES you should have recognized, understood, embraced, and become familiar with your emotional complex. In this phase, we will try to change your thoughts and feelings around your project. Although the instructions below mainly refer to mental compounds that can be addressed more effectively by reprogramming our brains, most natural compounds can also be applied. In the majority of cases, physical complexes can require specific and measurable behavior, e.g., with acne complexes, the person may seek medical treatment or alter eating habits.

Follow the following guidelines: The most important thing is to agree that it is time for your complex to be stopped and dedicated to it.

Defines the specific aspects of your complex that you would like to change based on the features of your compound (some elements of it may not harm your conduct and emotions). You can have real actions and measurable results in a specific context by being precise.

Develop a new perspective on your complex through the modification of the points in STEP 4 relevant to the old attitude and the creation of a new list of your current empowerment points. For example, your old view that' people believe that I am a failure and expect myself to fail' can be' I accomplish all the tasks I perform successfully.' Place next to each other the old and the new chart.

Another compelling and effective strategy is to start with your new releasing emotion by resolving your complex. The principal idea behind this is that it is much easier to achieve if you have the passion inside you first (even when you have to felt it), as it will lead you in that direction. For example, if you want to resolve your thin voice complex by exploring more masculine, start with the emotion of masculinity that a thick voice will offer you (even if you have to make it fake) and allow it to lead you in overcoming your voice complex.

VI. EMBEDDING THE NEW PERSPECTIVE INTO YOUR LIFE in this final step, the new perspective on the complex you have built and described in step 5 has to be mounted. Reprogramming your brain into a dilemma that has been torturing the mind for many years with a new collection of ideas, feelings, and behaviors is a complicated process and may take a long time. Nevertheless, once you have reprogrammed your mind and your new perspective, you have overcome your uncertainty and become free to do so.

The following methods should be used for optimal results: imagine, feel, and link the new perspective with pictures. Visualization is an advanced strategy that transforms the emotions. Success is first mentally produced, and the mind is our best tool, so use it to pursue your dreams wisely. For example, if you have a high-rise complex and your new perspective includes the perception that short people are as attractive and compelling as significant people, seek to imagine yourself in various situations in your present height as a beautiful and powerful person.

Use as your argument the list of points of your new perspective that you have built-in STEP 5. Affirmations are positive words that you say to yourself several times to mount them in your unconscious and configure your mind in the way you wish. You can type in your card list, place it on your computer, make audio recordings and repeat them when you have time. Try to relax before repeating your comments for productive dissemination (you should start using meditation techniques for relaxation).

Track your progress regularly, and see if you are on the right track to solve your complex. Use your emotions as a reference. If you see no significant changes, go again and consider revising your new viewpoint or modifying some of the strategies you have developed to suit your occasion.

You are going into an unknown mental area on a path towards the end of your psychological system, where you might feel fear, resistance, and other related emotions. Respect these feelings and respect them, obey your urge to free your complex, and let it guide you through your life.

Meeting Our Dark Side Benefits

To psychology, the name Shadow is given to a part of our own selves. This Shadow is our dark impulses, our "dark side," so that we speak— a hidden part of ourselves which we don't even want to show to ourselves. We may not know this—we may also be afraid to face it. But for the following benefits, it is best to visit our dark side.

- You can use your creativity and imagination to identify your own disowned portion. Some Shadow exploration activities focus on drawing, mind mapping, and the like. Associations with our artistic side will strengthen our link with this hidden part of us all.

- Any relationship can be restored with respect to more honest self-examination and direct communication. Since individual relationships are impaired by secret garbage, the more you can see what you conceal, the more you can appreciate certainties that are broken or terminated without any apparent reason.

- You will understand for other people what you "plan," which then shapes some of our views on others. We also want to see what we expect of ourselves in others. Instead of understanding the other, we do "theories" about what the other is based on what we know about ourselves. We could almost automatically think, wonder, "What do I do if I were him?" This is indeed a good question if we know that he or she's asking and don't use the thought to judge one's acts or thoughts rashly.

- You will continue to be free of the shame and embarrassment that comes with our negative feelings and, of course, our misdeeds. Yes, we can see why the Catholic tradition of confession has a real psychological value. In all good ways, we must tackle our dark urges to be free from them.
- You can even disfigure any negative emotions that come unexpectedly as you go about your daily routine. We must reconcile ourselves with adverse events and circumstances that suddenly desolate us.
- You can get true acceptance, a complete self-awareness of who you are, and who you can be.

CHAPTER TWO

Dark Psychological Techniques to Get Your Ex Back

In Your Spell People try to get their ex back in all sorts of things, but sometimes they struggle. Dark psychological tactics will help you get your ex back in a matter of time. There are some strategies to get your ex back, but they should be applied to achieve good results systematically.

We all face distressing times once in a while, and the most disturbing thing in life is when your lover leaves you. There are many ways to get your ex back over time, but some persistence is needed. Try not too desperate to save your relationship and make every effort to get your ex back.

Here are the Dark Psychological Strategies:

- Ask for your sense of curiosity. In all our make-ups, interest is a great driver. Individuals will do what they want to satisfy their curiosity.

- Wake up their curiosity in themselves. Self-interest is in us all a great motivator. Many are going to the ends of the earth to reward their own interests.

Do not run blindly to get your ex back. Prepare a stupid proof document for your husband. A systematic approach will only help you reach your targets. Be emotionally and mentally prepared first, and then start the strategy that you have in mind. Take time to get to your ex because hurrying won't solve your problem.

Trust the steps you take to get your ex back. Enthusiasm in the right direction will only help you get out of your situation. Systematically approach your ex with your qualified plan. Your friends will also help you solve your dilemma because they can love you and hold you constant.

Try to talk freely to your ex and also try not to hide things. The point-to-point dialog can help you solve the problem only. Remember to do what your ex likes during your meeting, and the chances to solve the problem will also increase. Stay relaxed when you refer to your ex. Therefore, these are some things to remember when you go to the next level.

How to Influence People with the Subconscious MIND?

You can find it easier to influence people, make friends, and resolve problems with the strength of the unconscious mind. Everything describes the way you program your mind to work. Below are ways to beat and stay a step ahead of the competition.

• Build relationships if you create connections with someone, and your subconscious mind will feel as if there is a specific relationship with you. This can quickly be done using the mirror technique; moving at the same pace or subtly copying their movements and places in the body can make you feel more confident in your conversation. Over time and with adequate training, your own subconscious mind will always try to reflect in an unobtrusive manner, and you can quickly build up relationships.

• Trust your intuition, Chess Grandmasters, as they can rely on their intuition, are capable of defeating even the most sophisticated chess computers.

This is not only a thought but a hunch built from past experiences to help you to consider what would be the next best move. Your intuition is based on knowledge and skills, so let your intuition be supported and trusted!

It is not true that loving or disliking someone is a random and uncontrollable event.

•   Dispel Myths about making friends in reality, and it is easy to make someone like you because the emotions of liking someone are controlled by the mind. You will find it easier to incorporate the small methods that will allow you to move forward by making the right connections in the right place if you understand and accept that.

•   Call for what they often want when they are looking for friends or trustees, people are trying to find someone similar to themselves, and yet they have something else to do. Professionals are, for example, inclusive of people who are equally qualified in the same field but also have excellent knowledge in another area or who have a higher capacity for leadership. They would, therefore, like to recognize the characteristics that most people want to achieve and consciously show, such as self-confidence.

- Place yourself in a mirror or look at a group of close friends objectively. Tell them in a few terms how they'd describe you. Do you want to be seen by others like this? If not, now take active steps to change your status. If you can put yourself correctly, it's easier to gain your boss ' attention or step up from the competition for this next promotion!

From the above strategies, it was evident that preparing the mind has many advantages. Through practice, you will discover a subconscious pattern that you represent or suppress as you communicate with others.

Where Is Your Mind and Your Heart?

It seems like a simple question, don't you? The easy answer is that your heart and mind is in your chest. After all, if you have a deep connection with something, you always feel it in your head because that's where you think deeper. And you probably think your conscience in your mind when you think, because it seems that this is the root of your thoughts.

Chest heart, head mind, and that are it. These undeniable facts are all you need to know, but reality has some more significant surprises for you. This is because heart and mind are fuel, and that opens a fascinating gateway.

There is something curious about energies where— they need not have a particular place — voltages can occur anywhere. Could that mean you can have access to heart and mind energies everywhere and wherever?

What is the power of nature?

Compared to things, let's explore this idea of energy or qualities. The power or value is something you can feel anywhere— rather than the thing itself; it's a state or characteristic. For example, a specific apple is red, but it can be read anywhere. Red is the price, but an apple is in one place—it's one thing. Yet what has this to do with you?

The physical heart is in one place, just as there exists in one place the physical brain. But the energetic qualities of heart and mind— not objects— are vibrations. You know that energy qualities are not limited to one location. Could it be that heart and mind qualities exist in every cell of your body? Can any atom of your aura bear the inner vibration of love and wisdom?

Such questions can only be answered through your own internal spiritual experiences. Can tell you about everything, but only through your personal experience can you prove it to yourself. But that's just how much with spiritual reality you can only verify through your inner realization, regardless of how many people insist on something being real.

Heart and mind are more than just feeling and thought, above thinking and feeling. They have profound, mysterious essences in you that vibrate in you as a living consciousness. Your very body is for your soul, a sacred temple, and your soul is made of the substance of God. Your divine soul holds in every particle of itself the energies of cosmic love and cosmic wisdom.

When you realize that in every part of your body, the energies or qualities of love and wisdom are felt or sensed, the famous statement that you are a spiritual being with human experience is understood.

Your body is a live tuning fork that is divine truth-sensitive. This is why the old advice to find the truth in you. Your inner fork is tuning to your soul's deeper essence, what many call your higher self.

In every part of you, there are the essential qualities that you identify with the Divine Heart: spiritual reality or merely emotional. The universal heart is not only the heart that feels the truth of something; it's a consciousness that perceives the heart that can be felt within each part of you.

The heart knows the highest truth of all it meets in its depths. The deeper core–the value of your whole being's spiritual soul–understands without thought and contemplation. But this only refers to the deeper essence of the soul.

The superficial aspects of the heart can be fooled by an emotional appeal. It is not possible to fool only the deeper essence of the spirit. This is why politicians know how to repeat simple slogans that hit the surface heart's emotions. They create fuzzy images of optimistic imagination, rather than offer real-life policy proposals. Publicity and media often also generate disappointing fantasies.

In each part of you, there are multidimensional minds: metaphysical reality–or only rational, the spiritual consciousness, the attributes which you identify with the Divine Mind. It's not just your brain that is able to know. It is the cosmic insight— the more in-depth knowledge of the truth— which can be recognized in every part of your being.

The body resonates in its very form with highest reality of whatsoever it encounters. The deeper soul knows this without analysis or thinking. It does this by finding harmony with the conventional spark within whatever it faces. But this only refers to the deeper meaning of the mind.

The information which seems rational in their assumptions but based on false or misleading information may deceive the superficial aspects of the mind. Media and Advertising often provide questionable facts that seem to indicate their point, so that the less issues of the memory can be directed towards the apparently logical conclusion and desire the product or a specific belief.

Have you noted the peculiar resemblance between the sincere heart and deep mind? Two sides of the same coin

• The knowledge of the real heart can detect truth through a deep sense of the essence of things.
• In-depth knowledge of the mind can discern the truth by thinking deeply about what is essential.

Well, that sounds almost the same, and that gives you a clue that both heart and mind are two facets of one greater truth at the deepest level — your capacity to fully understand reality.

The unexpected knowledge of heart and mind allows you to search the deeper levels of heart and mind, which reside far below the surface level of your being and can easily be tampered with. If you know this, you can release limited stereotypes about your heart and mind.

You notice that many spiritual teachings suggest that you feel the truth in your heart, but suggest that you do not have access to reality through your head. This may seem to be a harmless new age phenomenon, but it can create problems for those who literally take advice without searching for deeper understanding.

There is a significant disparity between profoundly affected heart experience and heart excitement. If you don't know the difference, they challenge you to grasp it all naturally and naively, without your more in-depth discernment.

It is natural to wonder because the students follow the curriculum sheep fully without asking a question, whether this simplistic notion of always following your heart fits other teachers and organizations. And if you ask questions, or if your conscience directs you other than the teachers, you are advised that you are unfaithful or that you are less religious.

It returns us to the idea that sincere heart–and deep mind–each have their way of accessing the facts. And you may find the profound truth in your heart and mind— as long as you go deep enough to transcend the surface illusions of your heart and soul.

Go deep within what single-mindedness? How are you opening the door to their secrets? And nevertheless, shouldn't mind be the eternal problem— the place to escape spiritual seekers? Well, did the creator just give you a mind to avoid it? Or is mind, like soul, a domain that has the infinite positive potential for you, if you learn to work with it?

The deep mind lives in a world without words, like a sincere heart. And deep thought, like profound soul, has a kind of harmony or continuity with what it meets; it knows the fundamental nature of things. This is an example of the difference between profound knowledge and shallow knowledge: deeper resonance of the truth gives you a sense of calm rather than excitement.

This is because there is tension on the surface of nature, where the more exceptional facets of mind and heart reside. This emotional surface stimulation is an emotional reaction to events that happen or appear to give the ego what it wants. The ego reaction produces some form of nervous tension, frequently mistaken for the facts. There is no friction when something is higher, and that is why you heard the still small voice of truth. It would otherwise be the fun, cracking sound of supposed reality.

A sense of gentle discovery when you approach your spiritual explorations with a sense of gentle discovery, it makes you easier to understand deeper realities. This does not interfere with the most profound developments in your wishes, expectations, and enthusiasm. And the deep delights that arise from your quiet observations exceed the mere excitement of the average spiritual experiences based on energy.

Superficial enthusiasm, easily generated, can seem a kind of truth for the surface heart. Nevertheless, passion and excitement can obscure the ability to discern the more profound truth within the soul.

The subconscious is also affected by anticipation. Superficial chains of logical thinking, which attract the mind, tend to point to reality. But these seemingly rational thoughts can be distorted, and the capacity of the deeper mind to perceive the real essence of a situation can be blurred. This is why apparently intelligent people may miss subtle indications; they were so caught in the tale twisted by the reasoning chain that they overlooked the forest for the trees as it were.

Yet deepness is not nervous, because it goes beyond emotional reactions, and is content to learn what it does. , it does not need stimulation, as it resounds with the truth of things, and that is deep-hearted and deep-minded. It is happy with reality and satisfied. In the heart and mind are at the core level of reality, due to these two peculiar attributes of heart and mind:

- The essence of the love of the soul is divine wisdom.
- Divine love is in the wisdom center of the soul.

Above emotion and reason if you want to bind your vital heart and mind, choose to touch your own sincere heart and mind with your spiritual inner communication. It's not enough just to hear about it. Nor can you feel the experience if you only hear a spiritual teacher tell you about it but encouraged. These internal realizations cannot be reinforced through appeals to emotion or reason as useful in other areas of life as these coping techniques can be.

Logic and emotion cannot reach the heart and mind's essence. This is because intuition and emotion drive you towards a solution typically, but don't align explicitly with the highest quality solutions. The rhythm and rhythm of heart and mind are essential at a sophisticated level outside the earthly realms of rationality and emotion.

The resonance has been shown that you know the first vibrating fork causes the second bifurcation to vibrate when you position a vibrating tuning fork near another fork of the same length. The first fork has no evidence to the second fork. The first fork must not motivate the second fork. The resonance occurs due to their similar ability to echo.

Degrees of truth in the same way as the two tuning forks, the basic knowledge of your heart and mind resonates with reality. But you may be more familiar with the earthy resonance types— necessary emotional energy or fundamental logical statements—and you may mistake this for a deeper understanding of your heart or mind. This is because the superficial echo makes you fool with its strong enthusiasm, emotionality, and passionate convictions.

Emotional reactions are, for example, a much-used resonance of lower quality in the media. This is how films make you cry, for example, even if you know it's a plot. You are absorbed in the story and understand the situation; music and lighting intensify it all and immediately emotionally respond. This is not necessarily a profound resonance of truth. But it shows you how easy the heart can be moved.

There is a pure, sacred space at the core of the heart and mind, beyond reason and emotions. You might claim it's just a sacred space. You consider a paradox in this space — mentalist is brain and heart is mind—it is known as facets of one another. Your goal is to gain access to those deep places within your being, to remember you are essential to nature and to be able to discern reality from worldly falsehood.

A vague inconsistency in the teachings of spirit

- Those who favor heart-oriented spirituality tend to stress emotionalism and blind faith— they play down thought and doubt.
- Those who prefer a religion that focuses on intellect tend to emphasize reason and cognitive control— they play down their senses and subtleties.
- Such inconsistencies lead to one disparity against another. Often when you see two directions that seem to be opposite, you are swept into confusion, and you assume you only have to choose one direction. But what if you have all paths unbalanced?

The third and better solution, which gives you more profound understanding and compassion When the nature of a person or circumstance is felt in the depth of the heart and intuitively understands the complexities of what is going on in the most profound mind, you feel compassion. It's different from empathy, compassion, or concern. And it's different from trying to fix the problem instantly. It is in-depth knowledge and understanding, and this kind of compassionate experience leads rather than quick-fixed responses to inspiring solutions.

Here are ways for the mind and heart to have higher love and awareness for somebody or something: how to reach the caring spirit of your soul: Deep mind wisdom is a profound affection for your contemplation's essential nature. This is different from just being fond of someone. By gently seeking the space in your head that transcends ordinary thought, you access mental love. Take advantage of your creativity to.

- Go deep into your head core.
- Go deeper; find the stage beyond logical thinking.
- Go deeper and find the only level.
- At this point, you can connect in a person or situation with the pure divine essence.

How to reach your caring, wise soul: in-depth knowledge of what you consider is the core of love of heart. You enter the wisdom of the heart by gently seeking the sacred space that transcends normal emotions in your body. Make use of the imagination.

- Go deep into your heart core.

- Deepen yourself and find the stage beyond emotional affection.
- Go deeper and find the only level.
- At this point, you can resound with a person or situation's pure essence.

How to go deep into your mind for the most considerable awareness of compassion:

- Bring your attention quietly inside, as if you were entering your inner light-just imagine.
- Imagine walking more in-depth into this inner light.
- Note—the inner light is in the body—you have the light of your sacred soul in every part of you.
- Relax in the light, breathe softly and allow the light to spread peacefully through your body.
- Enable yourself to do so without prejudice, judgment, or assumptions about how it should be.
- And every time you think there's something significant in yourself, it's just going deeper unconsciously because there are a sincere heart and a deep mind.

The gentle path to inner peace, compassion, and wisdom Maybe you are always wondering if you should choose to go deeper into your heart or into your head, as the debate about your heart versus your head is a trend of old. As you know, now, in your heart and your mind, there are countless deep layers of reality. You have the ability to use them.

An in-depth exploration of reality has little to do with anticipation, optimism, constructive thinking, or drama. , it is a quite deliberate choice to move your mind slowly into the sublime limitless depths of the universal self. Realize that enthusiasm and anticipation can be fun, but the noise obscures you'll find a more profound truth.

These transcendental states of love and knowledge have been written with profound spiritual poetry, but you must enter these secret places yourselves as moving and beautiful as possible.

The Almighty Maker, who made you, resides deeply within all his creations.

Divine existence, being infinite, has no definite form or set nature. To say that the heart is love is, therefore, minimal comprehension. Likewise, it is a limited understanding to suggest that the mind is knowledge. There is knowledge-love beyond wisdom and faith-wisdom beyond love. There is no tension between love and knowledge. And if they seem to be, you have still not reached your more in-depth level of perception of the particular situation where the conflict appears to exist.

And over and above these tags of love, kindness and knowledge is a secret room in which you know only that. The simple truth is always deep inside you, beyond language, reasoning, and emotions. But that's not what you're expecting and not as enjoyable or thrilling spiritually as you might think. But it is quietly sublime, not dramatically significant, as you may have realized; it is balanced cosmic simplicity.

May your explorations into the depths of your heart and mind bring you calm inner delight. When you slowly discover the deeper truths, the spiritual core of the universe resonates, and the eternal radiance shines within your infinite hearts and minds. Outside love, beyond logic and beyond poetry—the endless source of love and wisdom is your deep Centre.

How to Win Influence People and Friends?

Basic methods in people were handling. See how you rate them. Both in personal and business lives, they are invaluable.

- Criticism or accusation do not oppose, denounce, only alienates and sets others against you. He advises: "When we deal with people, let us note that we do not deal with rational creatures. We deal with emotional beings, prejudiced creatures who are guided by pride and ego.

Only think of an instance in which you knew this was real. What if someone questioned you, even if it was worth it, do you want to help or do something to make you happy? And did it cause you to retreat a little or get angry, mad, or sad?

The person accused tries to defend himself because he only sees things from his own viewpoint. Not theirs, but others are to blame.

The criticism is that people are cautious, hesitant, and hurt. The condition that had to be changed would inevitably remain.

In the case of studies, psychologists have shown that' animals rewarded for good behavior can learn much quicker and maintain much more effectively than an animal punished for bad behavior.

The goal of all of us should be to promote definite, self-control, and great character. A great man (or woman) displays greatness in handling small men.'

Some people are living to complain about it. Those consumers who call or email only want to complain, or you may have kids and have not already done what you asked ten times. You must determine for which type of person you want to be identified. Learn to be patient, understand, and' talk everybody's fine.'

- The point here is to offer honest and sincere appreciation that' the most significant impulse in human nature is the wish to be substantial.' You will have an immediate partnership when we can make people feel significant. Take the time to thank others, to acknowledge their contribution to something, and also to note what little others do about you—because you care about what they care—they are going to open their hearts to you!

The rare person who truly solves this famine of the heart holds people in the palm of his hand, and' she will even be sorry if the undertaking dies.'

One among the greatest assets is the opportunity to respect and inspire those around you. Be abundant in your appreciation and recognition of everybody you meet. Not in a fake, artificial way, but reach out and touch—a fantastic reward will come from it.

This is not flattering or self-motivated words to appease anyone but genuine appreciation and recognition. You could work in a cleaner's office, and you never stopped saying thank you. You will pass the receptionist or store check-out assistant and never spend the time feeling great. Such a simple thing will affect and support you wherever you go.

- The only way on Earth to affect others is to think about what they want and show them how to get it. The world is full of those who take and look after themselves so that the odd person trying to serve others selflessly has a considerable advantage.

You want to sell something to someone as a business owner. This is an excellent tip for your sales.

What is your customer looking for? What are they looking for in their words? If you can give them what they want, you will teach them how to do this, and your customers will have unlimited potential to help them find exactly what they are looking for — action springs from what we basically want.

Influence People at Work

As a leadership trainer, customers sometimes ask me how they can make more successful business decisions without becoming a' back-stabber' or an' ass-kisser.' There is a fine line between the display of corporate insight and the "dirty play" of office politics. Two terms make the main difference: motive and process. The chapter will provide you with strategies to help you become an expert in fine art while remaining true to the highest standards of professional ethics and values.

We have all seen the Black Art of Power in action: managers who suck up and kick down, who pay tribute to the efforts of others or leave behind burning staff. We know colleagues who always seem to have the boss ' ear and cause confusion by sowing suspicions. Or we have seasoned colleagues who frequently cross our heads due to their' specialized' skills.

In almost every case, the intention is self-serving, and the approach is ineffective. Influencing others becomes a Black Art if your purpose is to take advantage of everything to look good at the cost of others.

Individuals can sometimes persuade themselves that they have to use devious tactics because the cause is right. Methods can include presenting inaccurate or incomplete data, gaining from absences to limit opposition, outright lying, retention, or impeding progress. And the list continues. People may delude themselves that this conduct is right, particularly if they get away with it. Nonetheless, many know that the end does not justify the means.

Organizational flexibility and political skill are vital features that are successful in your job regardless of your rank. But, the further you go forward is especially crucial. You need help for your ideas not only from above but from below. You need the support of your colleagues throughout the organization and even those outside the organization.

In addition to added difficulty, the majority of large corporations have political and administrative decision-making levels. In government, elected officials and their legislative staff are at the political level; civil service is the organizational level. In business, the policy tier is composed of boards of directors and significant shareholders; the CEO and the staff are the administrative levels. This distinction must be recognized because each level has different perspectives and concerns. If you want your ideas accepted, you must take both of them into account.

Steps to boost people's ability to affect

- Recognize and recognize the key players.

Research the map of the company and current investors. Figure out who the decision-makers and power individuals are for your program or service and whose advice they rely on. Search for people who can help you understand players and positions at your stage.

- Learn to read the world politically.

Organizations may seem straightforward on the ground, but it's crucial not to underestimate their complexity because the people involved differing. See who is notorious for doing something, who are the guards, who control the flow of information and resources, who are the resisters and stoppers. Whose assistance do you need?

- Write between the corporate lines.

You must understand the context in which the organization works. You may not be able to get your idea endorsed, not because it is not successful, but because budgetary constraints or other considerations are more important at a political level in particular. Find ways to connect the program.

- Building partnerships at all stages.

Cooperate and support others as frequently as possible, regardless of their organizational level. You never know when someone is going to need to chat to you well or quickly. Don't hold grudges. Don't hold grudges. You will limit yourself later.

- Until presentation, meet stakeholders, check ideas, and develop support.

Go to the most hardened critic and get your feedback. Consult behind the scenes to solve problems and get help. When you find roadblocks, find ways to deal with them. This way, you can prevent strong vocal opposition, which can jeopardize your plan. So look out for fake consultation. When people give their opinions, please include them as well as possible. Explain why, if you can't. Nobody likes to be forgotten.

- Brush up your skills in conversation.

Pay attention to non-verbal signs of people, especially at meetings. Learn to consider the motives of others and listen to what is not said. Look at your vocabulary and adapt your approach to your audience. The older the viewer, the more succinct and concentrated it is.

- Be generous to your colleagues.

Everyone is playing in favor of the boss. You will see a win as a defeat to you. It is always prudent not to make this natural rivalry worse. Be open, share information, give credit, never blind them to meetings, and keep your self-promotion and ego under control.

- Engage the boss still.

The employer is the biggest asset and ally of yours. It doesn't matter whether or not you like your boss.

Understand the role your boss plays in your organization and help it achieve its goals. The manager is more likely to support your proposals.

- Stay flexible and polite.

A performance proposal can take time to develop, follow the process, and receive support. You must be flexible. Your plan can be made in much iteration to deal with all of the issues. Timing can also be a key factor. At the wrong time, a good idea will not get the publicity that it deserves. You may have to stop sometime to evaluate the landscape. Persistence is good. Persistence is good. It's not bulldozer or mosquito.

It's different for every organization. Knowing the environment and its function will help you navigate effectively through official opposition and even develop your ideas. In tandem with an open, frank, and thoughtful approach, you will soon master the fine art of power.

The Benefit of NPL

Are you stuck in a lock of the mental grid? NOW restart your brain with the help of incredible NLP training!

NLP is an understanding of the intelligence system in the brain. As Neuro-Linguistic Programming, NLP reads out. Therefore, the NLP approach helps to understand the interplay between neuro and language skills. The human brain is made up of neurons, and the NLP training techniques and concepts will program and reprogram these neurons accordingly.

NLP works on two primary principles. The presuppositions of all NLP models are

- Mind and existence are systematic processes- this theory states that all processes within a human body, which occur among human beings and the entire ecological system, are rational and methodical. Unable to isolate one part of the system from the other.
- The map is not the land–because they are one; humans only tend to understand the fact and

not reality itself. The theory seeks to differentiate an individual from a menu to a meal. It helps a person to know what they think and what they are. All in all, the technique maintains a person to extend the neuro-linguistic diagram.

NLP is both an art and a science. It tries to put the gathered data into effect. NLP learning has no sense without this practical application. NLP is a way to find yourself and thus to conquer one's cached negative attitudes and beliefs. The method was like a gift to thousands of people who had NLP learning and managed to overcome their doubts and different convictions. NLP's incredible techniques have helped to enhance their personal and professional relations and increase their confidence.

The origins of neuro-linguistic learning are hypnosis. Hypnosis NLP has evolved much earlier than NLP approaches today. NLP is basically a carefully designed way of thinking. The NLP practitioner tries to improve the areas of terror, desire, hate, or desolation. All in all, the excellent NLP methodology improves the overall quality of life of an individual.

NLP learning is typically performed in such a way that vivid anecdotes, success stories, and first-hand experiences are integrated. The markets are inundated with NLP books and newspapers. There are numerous websites offering free training and home study courses for NLP practitioners. These free NLP tutorials help a person to understand and master NLP's art, both conscious and unaware human behavior. However, the best way to understand NLP coaching is to work directly with a qualified NLP practitioner. There are also many institutions that hold neuro-linguistic training workshops and seminars.

CHAPTER THREE

How to Influence People to Reach Their Full POTENTIAL?

Being an influential leader means that you can enable others to reach their maximum extent. This notion creates mixed results for many rulers. New leaders will not give control to subordinates, dangerous leaders are afraid that a team member will surpass them in knowledge and skills, and authoritarian leaders will bear the burden of all decisions and actions until they are exhausted. Influent leaders understand that leadership is not a role, but only a title won for those who lead by their people's talents and strengths.

Most leaders claim that the gift of higher power and freedom is granted when promoted. Conversely, a name does not lead people to follow you, and it is hard to push a boulder up a hill without excellent leadership skills.

Leaders who choose to become a person others want to follow find a much more comfortable journey to leadership. It builds on a distributed business environment, accountability, and collaboration. Think of a mentor or coach, did they lead with authority, or did they motivate you, watch you grow and empower you to be your best person?

The greatest gift a director can give to himself, and his staff is to allow them to expand and grow, even though they may surpass their leader's capacity. So how can you allow others to reach their full potential?

Know your people, know their interests, abilities, talents, strengths, and wishes.

Not every worker represents their talents and abilities but acknowledges their skills and strengths and thinks about how to use them to optimize their ability. Identify personal and professional gaps and jointly develop a plan to address those gaps. Look at the holes you found. Are they differences in the quality of your workers, or do you consider a discrepancy that clearly shows the difference in your skills?

Please remember that you have been elevated to the manager; they have not, so it is not surprising that your workers have not the same expertise that you had before your promotion. Alternatively, recognize the talents, skills, and knowledge they have to do well (and feel satisfied personally) and improve those skills and skills. Always know that you can surpass your abilities as you grow your people and exclude yourself from studying current technologies. Don't be annoyed with this, but be proud to help them succeed.

Know that your job is to empower your employees.

Is an employee's quality short? How do you respond as your manager? Are you ready to fire an employee or tired of their failure to comply? As an influential manager, you also care for the well-being of your company. Did you know that hiring and training a new employee far exceeds the cost and time to change a team member's performance? Is this something you can afford in today's economy? Remember why you took the leadership role in the first place, to make your people work successfully in the organization. If someone doesn't do it, don't put them down by complaining or threatening to fire them. Anxiety and poor behavior never build. Concentrate instead on what works best, encourage them to use their strengths as they learn to improve the skills required to achieve excellence. Reward them for positive actions; let them know that through learning, you value them. Many parents would not raise their children to maturity if they had the option to abandon them for bad behaviors anytime, devote themselves to leading the role of a patient-led parent, a commitment reinforced by positive thinking.

Enable your team members to excel in their unique style.

Most workers communicate in some way with customers. Many have succeeded because of their personal integrity, some because they can improve ties and friendships, and others because of their technical skills. You want to please your clients, does it matter how this happens? Enjoy the unique nature of your staff and the gifts they have to offer personally. Recognize them before other men. Model recognition and praise so that your team members will use this skill together with others. Inspired excitement is infectious and can spread to workers and your customers and your company like a virus. Let the members of your team know that they work for a company that can make them happy.

The model is an animator.

Consider yourself a cheerleader; enhance your performance by positive encouragement and appreciation. Yes, we are as simple as Pavlov's dogs when it comes to it, we will always work for the prize.

Without your permission to succeed, and without appreciation, you rob your team members ' enthusiasm, dedication, and happiness, making your work harder. Is it not easier to compliment quickly than to meet after conferences, after trying to serve as an enforcer, to fire an employee you have been trying to change for months? What happens to other people's morals? The lack of support from one of its team members can bring a whole team down. If you model that allows an individual to excel, other team members also imitate this behavior, and each encourages the success of the other.

Hand over the wand of power.

"No manager has ever suffered from the power and productivity of its subordinates." Once people are able to make decisions to startup action and solve problems, they are durable. The Boeing 777 with 2000 Boeing employees was built in an aircraft hanger and asked what the company should do next. Teams work well together to determine how good performance looks and to identify specific goals, behavior, and metrics of success. Treat the employees as adults and use their shared intelligence to make choices that best serve the organization's interests. Leading does not mean that you need to control anything, turn over the wand of power, and see the magic happen.

Let others lead.

Leadership is not a position or a name. Leadership occurs at all levels. Employee engagement improves dramatically if workers lead. Does a team member who has a little more insight than others, who can easily and quickly win the support of the rest of the team? Feeling like a mutiny, would he just sit down speedily and hear your authority? Why not use this leader's capacity to delegate, challenge, and inspire the team? Leaders from all sectors bubble up to the top, let them lead from where they are, and will not only achieve excellent performance but will also have a positive impact on those that follow.

A position does not make for a leader since it makes people who follow because they want to develop a leader. Activate these six strategies to support your people, and you'll find that you're a popular leader, mentor, and guide who have not only a positive effect on your company but also helps the lives, trust, and skills of people you represent. Isn't that feeling better now?

Persuasive methods to Influence People

All of us live different lives, and there may be those of you out in your own community who go into battle every day. Therefore, here is a list of all the known persuasive methods that masters use to manipulate and get what they want.

Nonetheless, please note that great responsibility comes with high energy. Always use your experience and not just your own for the good of everyone. You're having that, Spidey?

How to Cooperate with People

- Humor-You makes people feel good if you can make them laugh. This allows you to build a relationship with them quickly.
- Smile-First impressions last, and first impressions with a smile are a benefit. Try to smile at every person in the street.
- Respect-We all know that it is appreciated and not hated. Firstly, however, you should always thank everyone you encounter. It's still convenient for someone who loves you to do a favor.

- Create quick connections-people who can immediately make contact with someone have more friends and can build good relationships than people who can't.
- Using body Language-Body language awareness is included in the program. Our regular contact is 55% body language. Although the people you talk with interpret the signals instinctively, learning how to identify such messages is an asset in the art of persuasion.
- The Halo Effect—Generally, we classify people as good or generally evil. Any characteristic that you will show a person in the future can be influenced by what you teach today. Make sure anybody you meet today feels like you're usually right.
- Similarity-Same feathered birds, don't they flock together? If you can always find a way to understand what is shared between you and the other person instantly, you can quickly build a connection. This relationship eventually becomes faith, which is always what people have to do for you.

- Goodwill-Be genuine always if you show interest in others. Being frank about your concern for others will make them quicker like you.

- Bonding–The names of people sound to their ears like jingle bells. Address people by name and they will pay more attention to you.

- The methods of mirroring and matching Mirror your language–Mirroring is a technique used for neurological programming to create relationships with an individual unconsciously. Using the same language, the other person uses will help you build this relationship in no time.

- Match your breathing–breathing alone can help you create a link that you are convinced to use. The effectiveness of this method is dependent on its disguise. Who will ever know that somebody is trying to copy their practice of breathing?

- Match the Tone-Matching, the voice of a person, operates on an unconscious level as you see all the mirrored techniques here.

- Mirror their moods–If your partner is in a bad mood, are you jokingly approaching them? Of course not. Of course not. Just assess the attitude of people until you do what you want.

- Test your energy level—The energy level of a person can tell you how likely you are to make suggestions. If you can be as cheerful or as energetic as they are, you can lead them to your plans much faster.

Cognitive dissonance test

- Create relationships—If you are able to get people to commit, this person will most likely do what you asked them to do. You will have a sense of uncomfortability that will last for some time if you don't.
- Using written Obligations-Written promises are better than oral ones. It can also function as a bond between you and the other person.
- Build public commitments-public commitments are even better than written promises. There will be not only a concern for the relationship but also the integrity of the individual.
- Using external rewards-business, people always use their workers' incentives. Although the in-

spiration it provides lasts only for a short time, it still does the job.

- Always make them say "Yes" –This is a kind of conditioning in which the response of the person is matched by the stimulus that you offer in this case.

- Make a concerted effort–if you can get people to make an effort, they will more likely stick to your plans or execute their requests.

- Create dissonance and offer a solution-just take care to provide a way out if you plan to make someone feel uncomfortable to get them to do as you like.

Create a sense of obligation

- Present Giving-How do you feel about giving a gift to someone and you've got nothing to give back? Very bad, isn't it? You'll probably say, "Geez, don't you have anything. Just let me know if you need anything..."

- Mutual compromise–Often, people will try to influence their minds, so that you may feel helpless when you know that you don't agree with what just happened. Don't worry! Don't worry! What the other person does not know is that when it is your turn to make him / her consent to your application, he or she is just as weak.

- Give a favor, get it back-people do things for you sometimes, whether you like it or not. The problem is that it induces a need to reciprocate in the mind of the receiver. If you are a generous person who is happy to give favors to others without anything in return, simply make sure you let them know.
- Sharing secrets-Share the secret to building a bond, a sense of duty, and a sense of trust. Just note, the secrets that you share depend on the type of person with whom you share them.

Group power think

- Build a team-The The more extensive the band, the better. Human beings have a substantial socializing need. People join groups to have a sense of belonging. If you want people to live up to your values, reinforce the community, and develop it.
- Familiarize everyone-if you can get people to identify strongly with your party, it will be easier to

influence their actions. Make sure everybody is the same as they think.

• Set the values–companies typically have beliefs that they bring together in the form of mission and vision statements. Such costs need to be adhered to by people within the organization or group.

The Scarcity Rule

• Illustrate the potential loss— the opportunity to lose someone or something can sometimes make us feel our freedom is limited. Often, when this happens, people act irrationally. If you sell a product or service, add a sense of potential loss and see how much it has to do with it.

• Tell them they can't-sometimes you wonder why you will want to get anything you can't have. It may have something to do with freedom of choice.

• Increasing demand; restricting supply–If demand for a product or service is high, people tend to flock to it. Consumers are always willing to buy what is on sale.

• Create an appeal-create an appeal by making yourself unique to generate interest in you or in what you have. Surround yourself with fantastic things and an excellent company to attract more people.

- Show Exclusivity-You are already exclusive if you follow the previous suggestion. People can't get to you, and they have to overcome obstacles (if you want to call it). The sheer effort to reach you will convince you that they will do anything to satisfy you.

- Announce a deadline-your biggest enemy is Procrastination. To ensure that your applications or directions are fulfilled when you want them to be finished, always set a deadline.

- Limit your freedom-the desire of a person always influences your behavior. Once you tell people that they can't get anything, the more they cry out for it. Believe me, and this trick is one of the presidents ' favorites.

The Persuasion Language

- Using repeated language-avoid using offensive words and replacing them with less offensive ones. For example: use mentally challenged rather than communication, idiot, propaganda, instead of torture, enhanced interrogation, etc.

• Play with Numbers-Play with numbers while you illustrate something to convince. Seek anything like, "close to nine in ten" or "less than five in all..." 38. Using positive words— what you want is for people to feel comfortable and confident in what they want. So, when you try to communicate, use positive words.

• Words with emotion–Words filled with emotions are incredibly helpful for people to behave. Only look at how the term "terrorism" was used by George W. Bush in his war against the enemies of America. Be quiet-the best thing to do after making a contract is to be silent. The person has already chosen, and you won't want to ruin the whole thing by giving the other man contradictory ideas by accident.

• Painting images with Words-Isn't it nice to walk around the park with the beautiful trees all over the place, swinging back and forth to the fresh air? You can only feel the morning sun's rays hit your soft skin softly before you stand on a pile of dog poo

(Hey! We just smash you. We're not even in the middle of the list)

- Choose the right words-The the right words will make a big difference sometimes. Instead of uttering, "Sir, I'm very sure we will have difficulty convincing your staff." Try this, "Sir, I am sure the workers will appreciate it and will give you more support if we try other forms." Replace "you" with "let's"—more people will participate by replacing "let's" with "you." The term "let us" gives you a sense of engagement. So from now on, let's try using "let's."

- Use simple statements-In simple, direct, and short statements; give your instructions. It's easier not only to remember but also to understand and absorb.

- Use your everyday language-your listeners and/or readers will only be fooled by complicated language. You have an enormous vocabulary, definitely, but if you speak like an intellectually dexterous (geek) person all the time, you will be misinterpreted more likely.

- Avoid vulgar words and curse words-try to prevent profanity in your comments (especially new acquaintances) as far as possible. Your reputation depends most of the time on the sort of terms you use.

- Avoid jargon, and technical Language-There is no problem when the person you talk to works in the same field you are in. Nonetheless, you communicate with different people in most situations.

- Keep phrases brief–A single phrase can stand as a whole in the early centuries. Today, we clearly live in a world where a single word like "party" is sufficient to say it all. This said, "Let's" "run."

- Don't beat around the bush-say it clearly if you have something to say.

- Using words–Words in speech are more likely to move people. Keep in mind that your words are conceived by the person with whom you speak. Thought takes precedence over motion.

- Terms like Free, Easy, Earn Now, Sexy, And Guaranteed are just a few of the other attentiveness terms that you can use. Try to Experiment these words in your statements.

- Highlight what you want-look at the last sentence above.

- Pace–Research has shown that speaking faster is more persuasive than talking slowly and monotonously.

- Avoid vocal Fillers-What does this mean... Uhm. To make ...Uhm. Your thoughts accepted. When speaking, don't use these kinds of words.

- Determine your pitch-it has been more effective for convincing speech to lower the pitch of your voice.

- Change the Voice-Speak loud enough to listen to you. Check the sound system first if you speak to a crowd so that the audience doesn't end up being deaf during your speech.

- Be more concise–concepts conveyed easily and regularly add credibility. People will most likely respond to your questions or orders if they can understand fully what you want to say.

- Taking a while to take a break— emphasis does not mean that you should talk louder, more quickly, in a low voice, etc. Sometimes you have to pause so that people have time to digest what you just said.

Distinguishing and comparing

- Triple value-if you sell a product, people will buy it more often when they see an additional value. Everything you offer, try to add a discount, bonus items, a coupon, or something else that gives a good impression.

- Change their perspective-try to observe how they break the price of what they sell into ridiculously small, manageable monthly payments when you talk to a salesperson. This is referred to as reframing.

- Switch focus–this is a tactic used by marketers to focus your attention on the "color" side of the image. Is the glass half full or half vacant? Is it wrong for your bag or suitable for your health?

- The door-in - the-face-make a big initial application, which may be denied. Make another request after receiving the answer, which is reasonable for the other person.

- Using Contrast-Another marketing form. Sure, you see a lot of this on TV. You compare your item or ask for something similar but unwanted to get the person to agree with you.

- Start high with your application—If you ask for a request, try to get a "yes" by starting high. Broad claims are typical "no," so make sure to first ask for something smaller before you get to the actual request.
- Use the appropriate timing—To make the previous technique efficient; always specify your real request immediately after the last method.
- Take note of the situation—are you in your workplace, school, band, church, or bar? Various locations have different moods. Be aware of the case to match the spirit of the person.

Suggestion Capacity

- Hope to effect-expectation is a prediction that fulfills itself. Did you know that you can only affect the behavior of people by telling them your expectations?
- Find over! Think done! Probably before, you heard this. But you shouldn't be the one to say this. Imagine the other person who speaks these words to give strength to your subconscious signals if you submit them.

- Using compelling advice-not only doctors who can use the placebo effect. You can do what you want people to do with the same idea.
- Emphasize the Time-How long, is it? Well, instead of the other way, it's time for you to make people do what you want. Did you get the point? Did you get the end?
- Use your name-most people strongly remember their credibility. "I know you're a generous man, Sir. How about raising me?"
- Using embedded commands-This is an example of an integrated command: "You should test that directly after you finish reading. Embedded command:" Test the one right away."
- Touching and leading-make the person feel comfortable and in agreement. Try to move them in the direction they want.
- Using role-playing-celebrities often have trouble with their positions. Pretending is a simple way to change your convictions. Pretend people and you can reach their subconscious minds.

- Ask for advice from people-Another way to involve people is by asking for information. Many people will even show you how to do it properly.

- Visualization-People who sell vehicles can give a potential customer a test ride. Probably, you are more inclined to buy if you can see yourself driving a car more vividly.

- Have a human contact-If you own a shop, it's more likely to sell than just stand around next to your cash deposit box and to chat with your customers friendly.

- Creating atmosphere-Many forms of business establishments use visual appeal, fragrance, and music to create an atmosphere and attract more customers.

- Creating Tension-There must be a relief if tension is present. Just as the plot in a film or a book, create tension, and eventually deliver a resolution.

- Allow hands-on experience–Computer software companies release beta versions of their products not only to test, but they also purchase the final version from customers.

- Learn how to deal with complaints-face it. You won't always be able to get people to agree with you, but you won't be able to run from your charm if you know how to deal with opposition.
- Tell contradictory stories-If you can tell your listeners or readers exciting stories, the more often you will be given attention and the chance to convince.
- Repeat use-advertisers know that your brand's single exposure on TV isn't adequate. That is why they show the product consistently to push it deeper into your mind. You should do the same with your feelings. Drive it further into the minds of other people.
- Repackage the message— you can use repeat, but you don't want people to take you or your ideas as a matter of course. Know how to repackage your post just like client repackages.
- Suspense building-Isn't it difficult to leave something unfinished? How about seeing the word "to be continued..." in your TV series? In reality, it keeps people returning for more.

- Create a Competition-There needs to be a rivalry to make people loyal to your brand or team. Build them vs. us environment.
- Engage the five senses–the five senses move through what reaches our consciousness. Seek to activate the five senses as much as you can by educating other people with the techniques described above.

Attention to the men

- Show new and innovative concepts-If you know how to recycle and repackage, you should also occasionally deliver something new. Now there are more options than before. When they find something better, they will leave you quickly. Don't give them that chance. Don't give them that chance.
- Using quotations-" Our appetites, our fears, and above all, our pride are the true persuader. The skillful propaganda pushes and directs these intimate persuaders. Create surprising comments –watch the primetime news, and in no time, you can know how to do this.
-

- Provide sufficient examples.
- Give solutions and advice-people want things that will make their lives easier and need them. With this game we call life, we all had it. Why not share something that is good for everyone.
- Know the art of questioning —questioning is indeed an art. When you learn how to use it properly, you can quickly enter the minds of others. Try these techniques of interrogation.
- Tell Them-Yours not the only one to ask questions. If people don't know, they don't want to. Have you any questions?

Like Using Flattery

- Favoritism at its highest Level-Favoritism at work is definitely expected. Show someone your favorite in every position, and you are sure you will get them to do stuff for you.
- Challenge the ego of the individual–have you the courage to try all that you read here? Let's see! Let's see!
- Don't react; just reply–you don't have persuasion. It's all about your goal, and your goal is to affect

others. Failure is sometimes inevitable, but dusts it off and moves on once you have learned your lesson.

- Make them feel important-it's an instrumental technique of persuasion to get people to feel self-esteem necessary. Give them an essential supply; they will give you a number of favors.

- Learn how to praise—apart from making them "look" significant, you need to tell people explicitly about them.

- Express appreciation—Any effort taken by the other person should be met with gratitude and appreciation.

Report Usage Association

- Using Permissions-You don't always have to work alone. Persuasion frequently requires the support of others. Companies rely on famous celebrities for their items. Find out how you can capitalize on your relationship with people with good reputations.

- Use the Anchor Method to learn how you can use the anchor method to manipulate feelings and memories of events, places, and things in the minds of others. The right kind of stimulation in the right environment is a useful tool for persuasion.

- Using signs and symbols-everywhere, you see them. See how many signs and symbols you can find all-around your house. You can try to study semiotics if you want to take this seriously.

- Salespeople bring their customers for lunch or dinner. Positive experience. Many businessmen do the same. Why? Why? So you can remember them. It's like your girlfriend on a first date.

- Patronage—Many companies sponsor different events to create positive associations. If you are watching sports, look at the banners throughout the stadium and see which organizations they represent.

- Produce enduring Images-Famous celebrities use various types of images to portray the characteristics that viewers want to experience. Have you ever tried to wear bling?

- Using colors-there is many different color definitions. You can use this knowledge to create a particular atmosphere or feeling once you know what each color represents. Let's try to find out how to handle emotions.

You are using feelings to take over them.

- Envy–Envy is what a person feels when he feels a lack of the attributes, successes, or material possessions of other people in itself. Nevertheless, to make someone believe jealousy is unwelcome, but still has an effective technique of persuasion.
- Worry-persuasion can be counterproductive if you are worried about something. Help the person to get back to reality by using positive words before using any of the techniques.
- Fear–Fear is widely used as a marketing strategy, but with your words, you can also convince people by invoking fear.
- Anger-Angry person maybe someone who wants attention. Anger. You just need to learn how to disperse the rage of a person when it's time for you to persuade.
- Sympathy-You sees that this is used several times on TV. Hungry children, tortured animals, victims of war, etc. When people are sympathetic to something, they are more willing to help.

- Envy–envy is what you get when you see someone else has something you don't want. There's a good chance you can convince a jealous person.
- Shame-When you do something you regret, you may or may not be able to make up for your mistakes. Help them get up if they still see a little hope.
- Pity–Pity is what you feel for the unfairly treated or unfortunate events you have seen in your lives.

Facts and Figures are used.

- Cite empirical studies-if scientific evidence supports you, and people are more inclined to believe your argument. Often adding the words "scientific results have proved..." will make an essential difference in your vocabulary.
- Collecting Evidence-There is a reason why we look at product reviews, movie reviews, book reviews, etc. The more proof you can provide, the more you contribute to the argument or claim for your brand.

- Data on Using maps, graphs, and data, etc. All of them have figures that will help you provide your listeners or readers with stronger evidence.
- Create a metaphor — sometimes, for a long time, you can describe it, but people cannot understand it yet. The use of analogies is like watching a theatre version of a book.
- Show published Reports-You can use them to support your complaint if it is documented or published in a newspaper.

Exploring Mind Control History and Programming

Anyone who has ever wondered how the human brain could be controlled will find plenty of knowledge about the issue. Innumerable people feel the context behind the thought manipulation is fascinating. While numerous individuals may dismiss the subject as science fiction, many others believe that different governments in countries around the world have used thought manipulation. In contrast, some religious movements and societies may have changed their philosophy.

If a person wants to understand the concept of thought reform, it is probably a good idea to examine this topic in detail. One way to start such research is to explore the history of mind control and programming. There is a lot of information about how intelligent manipulation might have grown. It is also interesting to consider how various individuals, organizations, and associations have made use of thought reform.

One phrase widely used with this subject is the word brainwashing. The root of the word can be traced, brainwashing. The term has been used to refer to the thought reform that the Chinese government may have implemented against certain people, such as US military personnel held captive. These prisoners may have complied with their captors ' requests. This behavior may be attributable to brainwashing. In some cases, prisoners have become loyal to the Chinese government, rather than the government of the United States.

Many people think that during the Korean War, the Korean government brainwashed American soldiers.

Nevertheless, after a great deal of research on the subject, the US Army officially denied that this is accurate and provided no proof that brainwashing was used. The correct assumption on this subject seems to be that such a strategy was not used by the North Korean government for American prisoners of war.

In 1950, its own brainwashing system was established by the Central Intelligence Agency of the United States. This behavior mirrored the fact that other governments were also experimenting with this method. In an effort to remain unbeaten in hostage thinking, the Central Intelligence Agency, commonly known as the CIA, investigated the issue of brainwashing. Most people believe that the CIA has been conducting research on a deep level for decades.

Government agencies definitely are not the only institutions that have been known to experiment with brainwashing. Different religious groups and cultures have also used thinking reform as a way to manipulate people. Customs and religious movements have carried out considering manipulation in the United States since the 1960s. One common form of thinking change is to disassociate people from their families, families, and colleagues at a spiritual level. In so doing, rulers and other cult members will exploit people far better than if they were in close contact with those who care for them.

Six conditions can make a person susceptible to thinking reform. The first step is to make sure a person does not know that anything unusual happens. The second step describes the development of a fully controlled and segregated physical and social environment. The third step is to make the oppressed person feel helpless. The fourth step is to exploit the person's previous actions and lifestyle through punishment and reward. The fifth step includes the application of incentive and discipline as a way to attract the team and its values. The sixth and final step is to assert absolute authority over the individual deceived by the religion.

Although many people feel that the modification of thinking has only been used in a negative way, many others agree that the method can also be used to achieve good results. Many view hypnosis as a form of mind control and many have used hypnosis to alter unhealthy behavioral patterns. Hypnosis is used to help people stop smoking, lose weight, change their career paths, and discover their personal achievement. Hypnosis could also be used to modify thought mistakes, control frustration, and reduce anxiety. Some people have had great success with anesthesia, so it can be possible to make successful use of mental control.

Guided imaging is another technique that can be described as thought manipulation. This procedure is often done in a therapy clinic and is usually followed by a counselor. This technique can help a person turn negative patterns of thought into positive ones. As a consequence, a person may change a number of behaviors and opinions which are detrimental to physical, mental, or emotional well-being.

The theory of thought reform is certainly not new, but it is as exciting today as it was when it first became publicly known. Exploring the subject of brainwashing is probably suitable for almost anyone. Individuals who are amazing may want to know about thought change so that they are not exploited at some point in their lives against their will. If you're going to use thinking to improve yourself and your experience, you can find a wide range of professionals to help you with such work.

Want to find out more about mind control and programming exploration and other great topics?

Mind control is thought reform, manipulation, brainwashing, coercive control, mind control, coercive persuasion, malignant use of group dynamics, and much more is also known as mind control. The lack of a common name implies misunderstanding and manipulation (most especially through those who use it hidden for own benefit!!) Let us accept that mind control falls under the umbrella of persuasion and power—how to alter the attitudes and behaviors.

Some argue that all is manipulation. Nevertheless, essential distinctions are overlooked in saying this. Influence is much more valuable as a continuum. On one side, we have moral and fair values that respect people and their rights. On the other end, we have disruptive forces that strip people of their individuality, autonomy, and potential for rational or logical thinking.

It is for this reason that we consider divisive religion and sects. These groups use disappointment and tactics of mind control to take advantage of the weaknesses and forces of their members to satisfy the needs and wishes of the religious leaders themselves.

A cult of one person is an intimate relationship in which one person abuses the influence of his or her manipulating and abusing the other, e.g., teacher or student, therapist or client, pastor or worshipper, wife, or wife. This cultic relationship is a variant of the larger groups and maybe even more damaging because one person is always involved.

So what is mining?

It is better to consider it as a set of forces that greatly disturb an individual at the very heart of his or her identity (its principles, beliefs, desires, decisions, attitudes, relationships, etc.), creating a new pseudo-identity or pseudo-personality.

It can, of course, be used in good ways, for example, for addiction, but we speak about inherently wrong or immoral conditions.

Psychologist says that mind control is "a mechanism through which personal and collective freedoms of choice and action are jeopardized by agents or agencies that change or distort perceptions, motivation, results, awareness and/or behavioral effects."

It's not an old mystery known to a few, but a mixture of word and group pressure, designed to make a manipulator dependent on his followers, taking their decisions while encouraging them to believe they are independent and free to decide. The person influenced by the mind is not aware of the process of manipulation, or of the changes taking place in himself.

Distinctions Essential!

Many vital points must be made very clear.

First and foremost, it's an insidious and subtle process; subtle that means that the people are not known of how far they are affected. Therefore, they make small changes over time, assuming they decide for themselves when all the decisions are taken on their behalf. Insidious because it's meant to catch and harm.

And it's a phase because it doesn't happen at once. This takes time, but the length of time depends on the tactics used, manipulator's capacity, the length of the techniques ' exposure, and other social and personal factors. Manipulators are now skilled enough to occur within a few hours.

Force is involved. Physical strength may exist or may not exist, but psychological and social power and stress are definitely present.

An exciting difference between mind control and brainwashing,

Mind control versus indoctrination.

The victim knows in brainwashing that the aggressor is an enemy. For example, prisoners of war know that a person who washes his brain and tortures is an enemy, and they often realize that staying alive depends on changing their beliefs. We are forced to do things that we usually would not do, often with physical strength. Nevertheless, when the victim avoids the enemy's control, the brainwashing symptoms always vanish.

Mind control is subtler and complicated because the manipulator is often considered a friend or instructor, so the victim doesn't try to defend herself. In reality, he or she may be a willing participant, and, assuming the manipulator has in mind his or her best interests, he or she frequently gives private information freely that is then used to keep control of his or her mind.

It makes mind control, if not more dangerous than physical coercion. In other words, torture, physical abuse, drugs, and so on can be even more useful. There can be no physical coercion or violence in mind control, but it can be far more effective in controlling a person.

That's because coercion will change behavior, but oppression (mind control) can change perceptions, values, modes of thinking, and actions (mainly changes in personality). And the' victim' participates willingly and positively in the changes and feels it is best for them!

So it is challenging to recognize and exploit someone you trusted and liked later, and it is one reason why it is not easy for people to understand mind control. Even when the perpetrator remains free to control his personality, the behaviors, opinions, and actions, mainly because the victims feel they have made these choices themselves (the consequences of our decisions are higher and longer-lasting than those we know that we have been encouraged to take).

You will learn more about the way all the changes are made by the mental control of narcissistic boyfriends and narcissistic men in this section.

A Gun to the Head

Manipulators like to say that nobody has a gun in the managing head, and this has two forces. It is difficult to argue with the outsider who does not grasp mind control.

They know that this is true for the manipulated person. Nobody has held a gun to his head, so it reinforces the idea that they chose for themselves. And our decisions are much stronger, and the effects last much longer so that the manipulated person furthermore profound into the reality of mind control.

Who's doing it?

Who would use these strategies to ruin other people lives for their own egoistic gain? And exploit others merely because they can or want control? Psychopaths, sociopaths, and narcissists are solutions. Most extreme manipulative men and women who use intelligent power probably fit the profile of a psychopath or a narcissist. And because they have no conscience, the reason they can do it!

Since people are unfamiliar with what a psychopath or narcissist is, the manipulator is often called something else, a woman abusive or a manipulated wife or husband, a jealous partner, a man verbally abusive, or a very strict supervisor. Closer examination also suggests a personality disorder for these individuals.

Twelve strategies Ways to Win Friends and Influence People

Have you ever been a new kid at school? Can you think the classmates look suspicious? Remember, you are trying hard to fit in? If you were a new employee, board member, volunteer, vendor, customer or director, the current staff, workers, boards, volunteers have probably felt the same fear. You might also recall trying too hard to fit in when things got worse. When a new person joins the team, they switch it. Whether or not the group likes it, and often it doesn't, it only changes as new people enter. An active team wants to be interrupted as little as possible. The more you do to make the change painless, the sooner you are welcome and able to contribute.

The current team may be afraid of:

a. The character will not align with the existing team

b. The new person will make improvements in the workings of the group

c. He will not understand or respect what was done and

d.   He does not recognize the culture of the people or group

e.   It takes too long to make decisions and assignments by not adopting team activities

f.   If a team works well together, they don't want a new person to interrupt their cohesion by asking too many questions, needing clarification for past decisions, or trying to supply information from their spoons.

The person was eager to get along with everyone and contribute quickly when she joined a project team. Although she had good intentions, she took so long to ask questions about the team decisions during the meetings that she couldn't participate and eventually left the team. While everyone enjoyed it, they didn't want to spend time at meetings rehabilitating everything that was already functioning. If a team does not work well and does not produce the required results and is about to collapse, a person may be asked or invited to join the team to repair them. In that case, the goals of the individual will vary from the purposes of the group. Conflicting goals can, however, also be a problem for effective teams. The targets of the newbie could include:

a. Create credibility immediately, so other people know that they are worthy of being part of the team.

b. She defines her function quickly, so she can dive first in her brain.

c. Personally, something new by reading or trying.

d. Networking to get business directly or as references from team members.

e. Make your mark on the group to further its goal as it feels best.

f. Realize for past run-ins with a team member or a team member.

g. Promote your own career by being part of the accomplishments of the team.

It would be wise for existing teams, boards, departments, and groups to have a structured introduction when new people join, but it is often up to the individual to identify the team and contribute rapidly.

The following twelve strategies can contribute more to new teammates than to disruptive teams:

I. Please be invited. Provide your strengths and support, but don't pressure a team. If the team wants you, they welcome you and include you enthusiastically.

II. Commit to the group goal. Know before joining before joining. If you don't buy-in and can't support the task, don't join the team.

III. Have a justification for wanting to be part of the team. Know what you're bringing to the group and how you can help the organization advance its goal. Don't just join a team to be part of a team. Joining for purely autonomous reasons or politics won't help you win friends and influence anyone.

IV. Respect history. Make respect history. Learn how and why the group was created, what it achieved, and who it was.

V. Get to know the people about their terms and conditions. Let them touch you. Let them reach you. Don't force yourself on them again. Learn and depend on their talents and contributions.

VI. Understand the culture and the interaction of men. Evaluation of friendships, forms of communication and interaction adjust with existing standards, traditions, and types.
VII. Know the principles of the squad. For example, one board can be warm, welcoming, gracious, and value-added, while the other can be formal, title-consent, and regulatory. It would be helpful to understand what board you enter so that the conduct is culturally compatible.
VIII. Understand the teammates ' formal and informal positions. Know who the representatives are and who works regardless of written policies. If you are a new team member, do not immediately change the beliefs of others, because you may not know the strengths of others and maybe resentful.

For example, when John was the new chairman of a board, he put up a list of the positions that he wanted in the roles he had filled. He left three main contributors out of the list, which effectively took them off the table. Earlier, when no-one on the board bought in because of their frustration at his big idea of the fundraiser, John called out two people and asked them to support his cause. The cause never got off the ground because John was so arrogant, and nothing substantial was done in his time.

IX. Read about processes, strategies, and decisions. One council, for example, makes decisions during meetings. You don't have a say in the choice if you skip the meeting. Everyone in the team knows this and is all right. If a new person cannot be present, he might want to postpone decisions, which will not go well with the group.

X. Learn more than you're talking about. Absorb through listening to community, procedures, history, individuals, politics, and roles. Ask questions when a meeting or momentum will not be interrupted. Listen to the team and adapt.

XI. Offer help. Offer to help. It is unwise to ask the team for favors like referrals, meeting location preferences, or changing the schedule when new. If you have joined the team for what you can do, the team can soon see that, and you won't be included.

XII. Relax. Relax. Take a foot first and then dive later. Scuba diving disrupts teams first and leads to resentment and often causes organizations to dissolve without fulfilling their objectives.

If invited to join a group, ask why you are invited. What do you need the team? What time, money, attendance, and other responsibilities and expectations are they? If you join the team, meet the person who, after the first meeting, extended the invitation again to discuss the 12 items above to help with your start.

Whether you are the newest employee, member of the board, volunteer, customer, seller, or teammate, you should anticipate specific fears, goals, and expectations. Take the initiative to be a valuable teammate by resisting the common temptation to dive firsthand. Instead, take a careful look and make friends, influence people, and make a useful contribution to the team and its mission.

Knowing THE WOMAN'S Mind

Were you ever itching to get into the mind of a woman and ask what she is thinking exactly? Well, mind reading isn't something you'll learn in this book (sorry if you expected). But most people are motivated by the same fundamental motivations, as you are about to learn. When you know what they are, you can communicate with nearly every woman.

Also, if you haven't realized it, women are different from us. It's like they're from a whole other world sometimes and they speak a different language. But it's not so difficult to understand people, and it's just different. Essentially, you need to understand the two primary ways women think differently from us.

- How women get their way does not influence others in the same way that men do. We can't. They can't. We are less vulnerable than we are physically, and that is why most people (and some women) believe that they can easily overcome a woman through bullying. If a woman wants to get her way, she has to use other tools. The most common is the manipulation of the emotions of people.

For example, when a woman gets fucked when you don't do what she wants, claiming that you "made her mad." No. No. She is a grown woman, and her emotions are controlled by her. However, men are real suckers for drama because they think they take responsibility for the emotional states of a woman. It does things (or does not) to avoid "making" a woman feel sad, stupid, jealous, upset, unsafe, furious, or other dramatic emotional states.

When you think about it, it's hilarious. A woman can overwhelm a man with drama literally. And who can blame them for this? For a very long time, it was their only choice. Not only physically are they weaker, but they have disadvantaged of authority for thousands of years and are compelled to use Further creative ways to show men's strength. And of course, you've noticed that they've made it a science.

Let's clarify something before we go on: there is nothing wrong with the use of drama or manipulating people to do it. All of us use manipulation to obtain what we want. Some people refer to it as inspiration or influence. But we never force the person to respond to us, in any case.

In fact, men are more likely than drama to use bullying to get what they want. So it doesn't make sense to hate women to use the scene to get what they want. Instead, we will use this information to increase your choices for enhancing your relationships with women.

And that's just beginning to understand this: you will never find a woman who is "free of drama." People are emotional because it's a way to get what they want, what you have to do as a man is to learn how to handle the drama and prevent women from using it to dominate you. And believe it or not, this is precisely what women want of a man.

• How Women Process Attraction If this last statement puzzles you, it will clear the confusion to understand how women attract. This starts with understanding the one thing about women that most men have totally backward: what women want in a man. First, if you ask women for advice on dating, that's right now because you'll just make yourself crazy. You might have worked this one out already.

Have you ever wondered why women don't seem to know what they want from a man's relationship? They say that they want a nice man who is good at treating a lady and who loves his wife. A sensitive man who opens the door to them asks them how beautiful they are and how wonderful a friend they are.

Instead, however.

We are madly in love with people who are unrefined, crazy, cocky, a little childish, and who you just look at and wonder: "How the hell is this guy doing for him?" You are, in the meantime, the good-natured man who knows how to treat a lady and who loves his wife. A guy who is compassionate and caring and opens her door tells her how beautiful and kind she is.

And where do you get that? She slowly writes you out of her life as either a "great friend" or worse.

What's that all about in the world? You did all according to the book. You were the guy she said she needed. Why did you get to the place of your wife after watching her fall over her head for that "other jerk??" That's because what the women want is not what they think they want. And the sooner you recognize this, the sooner you will quit trapped in the' Friends' Corridor.' Now you shouldn't be shocked.

After all, almost everyone does not claim that they want things that are entirely different from what their behavior reflects?

How many (men and women) do you know who is healthy, but who is consuming sugar-filled sweets, unhealthy fats, salt, and preservatives? How many people do you know who are wealthy, but who spend their money carelessly and who can't wait to go home to see TV throughout the day? This is because, while people want to be wealthy and safe, they are motivated by deeper motivations that most people don't take time to comprehend.

Don't tell people to judge. Many people are quite naive about the real reasons behind their actions, so they genuinely believe themselves when they tell you what they want. Yet look at their actions, if you want to know the real story.

Don't listen to what she says, if you want to know what women find attractive to look at her actions. Believe it or not, there's something "jerk" that most women like a flame moth.

They're making women feel safe and exciting.

This is an enticing mix because security and anticipation are two of the primary emotional needs people are looking for in romantic relations. If a man meets those two emotional requirements of a woman, he ignites a powerful unconscious attraction that transcends the reasoning mind of a woman.

Sound difficult to believe? Only think of how men you know who have given up thinking because of a woman's physical appeal. Think of how many people give up their thought and eat food they consider to be bad because they taste good. Think of how many people know who is spending their money on things which they don't need and end up having broken, and then buy lottery tickets as "they want to be rich." This is why "jerks" (we will call them Bad boys) spark unconscious causes of attraction that seem to contradict a woman's spoken desires.

How's that?

First, these "bad boys" are immune to drama control, making them unpredictable... which are exciting for women.

Think about that, how exciting is it to a woman when a man answers her with what he wants because he is afraid to make her feel sad, frustrated, jealous, angry, unsure, stupid, or some other dramatic emotional state?

It's pretty dull, as you can imagine. The more beautiful a woman is, the more acquainted she is with people who bow to her every time she uses drama to dominate them. And frankly, she's all right with most people because it gives her more power. She just doesn't date such men.

She dates the people who are able to take over and who are not frightened by the drama. And that's where security and security are needed.

Think of this: how comfortable does a woman feel when she has a partner she can present? Does that mean he is insecure, weak, and obedient or reliable and trustworthy? Obviously, many women would like to have a nice man who knows how to treat the lady and who loves his wife. A caring, responsible man who opens her door tells her how beautiful and a great friend she is.

But most men are either: the nice man they say women want or the unrefined bad boy. Exceptionally few people could be both, and as the Bad boy see her need for security and excitement, she selects him above the boring man of beauty.

Freedom of the Soul and Mind Intelligence

Attention, diversion, and true freedom Our Creator grants us freedom of thought. Our mind constructs our reality. Humanity as a whole has lost its ability to see the connection with aspects of consciousness, especially ideas and feelings and the experiences and conditions of our lives. We are now re-awakening to our real creative powers by Divine grace and intervention.

This is an opportunity to reassess our life and our environment and change anything that does not mirror our actual being. We should put the pain to an end. Poverty and debt can be stopped. We should put an end to delusions and suffering. We can enjoy optimal health.

Humanity as a whole and each one of us experiences cognitive dissonance or pressure individually when we are not aligned with our real mind power.

By realizing our inherent spiritual freedom, by how we can regain it, and by using its creative powers, we can be made free to create and experience our lives and our world according to the wishes of our pure hearts. We can experience plenty and accomplishment. We can draw on our soul's energy, know the truth, and actively direct our minds. We can discover our individual gifts and use the creative freedom of our birthright to put meaning and purpose in our lives. This is the Universal Order and will bring our world peace and harmony.

Our beliefs and knowledge have become distorted by societal conditioning. Our minds were like tennis balls, here and there, directed and redirected by external forces. We haven't held the strength of our minds and hearts consciousness. We have lost our individual sovereignty. We have diverted ourselves from purposeful living. We also established the belief that life happens to us instead of us. We also switched to the consciousness of the survivor.

The first idea to consider when the independence of the mind is re-established is conscious awareness. Typically, most of the time, we focus our attention outwardly. Unless we regularly meditate or contemplate, our consciousness observes the external reality. We must spend regular time concentrating our attention internally on the energy of our soul-our true self. We understand the facts by tapping into our inner wisdom. We are motivated by our intrinsic spiritual nature. We receive guidance and guidance for our lives and discover our individual gifts.

What we focus on is where our energy is going. It also schedules our memory. If we are mindful of what we do with our attention and its impact on our lives, we can be inspired to make some beneficial changes.

Social conditioning happened by design. Design; if we can be persuaded to give up our religious freedoms, others can govern us. You can use our personal power and fierily build up the precious resources of the world through selfish motives and disappointing strategies. It's been going on for a very long time. Technologies are used in harmful ways that destroy life on our planet rather than support it. There's plenty to be brought into our consciousness so we can rise above it. We will learn to achieve real ideals and use our broader internal technologies.

Our unconscious minds are conditioned intentionally by ads that involve subliminal messages and symbols. We have been programming values by making us believe that our being and that our worth depends on what we have. We manipulate our expectations to support the small rather than the common interest of the whole. Awakening to the facts about these things will help to reinforce the value of the improvements that we need to make to motivate ourselves again.

Geoengineering, prescription drug drive, propaganda media manipulation, environmental warfare, bio mark, radiation, and cell phone technology EMF waves that are meant to kill or ruin us have little influence over us because we master our own minds and vibrations. The frequencies of love have proven to improve health and well-being. Adapt to Earth frequencies by joining nature. Understand the Schumann health and well-being resonance factor. Your mind's going to answer. Your body's going to get healthy.

Distraction is a way to capture attention and energy. Entertainment Have you ever had a target or something to achieve and then distracted? What have you done to remove distractions to achieve your goal? Have you ever "set your mind" and done something?

Imagine removing all obstacles and concentrating on your desired results. Use your mind (attention), your heart (feelings of passion), and your body (physical action) to achieve your goal. Practice setting some goals and concentrating your attention. Inside you will sense the intrinsic value of being in harmony with your True Self (joy, happiness, peace).

Consciousness is not about ignoring the truth. This simply puts the results of what was created in the periphery of the mind into the causal structure of the mind and the whole consciousness, to produce something better. No, knowledge is reliable. By knowing what we will replace it, we can't just dwell on things that are negative. We are conscious makers.

True Freedom By concentrating on our inner core to our soul selves through our hearts with interior attention, we will experience true freedom. This attunement is a consciousness adjustment. It binds us to the genius inside. We know that we are the center of love Infinite, indivisible, complete.

It is time for mankind to regain control and be free of our minds consciously. Unable to continue suffering, unable to stay hidden oppressive powers and to try to control our thoughts for us.

We must choose wisely and work to regain control of our minds. This can be done by consciously looking toward, removing distractions, and concentrating our attention on solutions provided by the intelligence of the soul.

CONCLUSION

Mind control can be carried out only when the understanding of the mind's internal operations is obtained. This can be done by providing a subject with detailed information about themselves and/or by allowing psychologists to carry out in-depth examinations. This sort of heart and mind analysis is required to understand the criteria that regulate processes that govern the actions of a particular subject. You cannot start developing any system that drives a person until you fully understand how external stimuli stimulate them.

There are tools designed to control people or specific aspects of human behavior. A single device alone is not enough for the tasks required for mental control. Several phones must be used. The growing system will concentrate on a specific parameter type. These are not limited to emotional awareness and perception. Using these instruments, one can analyze how certain stimuli are responded to, record the results of the performance of the subjects, and use them to establish control specifications. The control spec is accurate only if the issue is in the same state as the spec. The stimuli produce different outputs as the only state changes.

If the subject is aware of the study, it will not be easy to collect data. A willing question may not perform very well, even if they want to cooperate. This is evident when you measure consciousness. This is clear. To obtain an accurate result from a subject, it must be in a grounded state or an average awareness level, indicating that the examinations are unaware of them. The output can only then be used to determine control requirements. There is no way to get a subject's agreement unless they know what they agree to. It can be possible to understand theoretically what the experiment is, but it undermines the validity of the study.

During the time mind control was developed, the technology needed for such experiments was not available without the subject. Today, particularly in the world of digital technology, several ways to pry an individual's heart and mind without their permission. The same innovation has also made it possible to create more powerful and effective intelligent control devices. Mind control devices should not be confused with traditional methods that people use every day. Mind control devices consist of different types of components, some of which are made from human hardware, others are social components that have specific functions that fit a particular subject, and chemicals are also standard components of these devices. A group of these components can be combined to work on a specific subject parameter. These are ideal tools not always connected by physical materials but by intent and collaboration. Many of these intelligent control devices can be created to submit certain input types of data that incite the subject to generate control specifications. These are carefully developed and maintained because they are costly and time-consuming.

When stimulated, each type of control parameter produces a different effect. The stimulation can be deliberate (performed by a human agency) or a result of relatively unintentional natural events. In most instances, certain external circumstances dominate.

What we want here is the power that a human entity initiates. The switch of one type of control influences the other and causes a dynamic change of state. A person of full consciousness attracts many external stimuli. Given the possible conditions, awareness of fully human consciousness may be almost impossible.

There are interferences to be addressed to gain reliable control over the mind. Natural phenomena often present problems during the mental inspection of adverse state changes. It is essential to filter this interference. Acquired control specifications obtained by the experimentation in a grounded state can only serve as the basis of the calculation of the deviation from the grounded state performance. Filtering can be achieved by manipulating the interpretation so that the subject is grounded. Measuring improvements make it more difficult for developmental control devices. Dynamic change in control parameters involves several qualified members or multifunctional members who can manage many changes in the system.

Mind control tests with individual subjects are not isolated. Small and large classes of humans, people, pets, plants, insects, other conscious objects which can be influenced by stimulants may be subjects used in these studies. For cases involving human subjects, the inherent respect for human life or freedom of choice is to be diminished. Those who finance behavioral health programs appear to be wealthy or have access to large amounts of money and see it as a valuable resource investment. A carnal desire for power lacks reverence in hearts for others, and the alien force of covetousness takes over. As a result, human rights are grossly violated, and all individuals, women, children, and other conscious creations in the world are affected.

The violation of privacy is at the heart of the practices involved in the development of intellectual power. Privacy infringement is an essential component required to obtain control specifications because a subject cannot be aware of the experiments. Projects relating to intelligent control will be postponed, canceled, or suspended as a result of information leaked concerning privacy violations. Those who announce preparations for human rights violations are regarded as dealers or dissidents. The power or authority to breach privacy is typically extracted from a global or national crisis. Such problems are being funded by people to make progress in command practices. Sometimes even disasters are created by members of their societies to strengthen human rights. The fight to violate human rights stems from those who raise society's awareness by disseminating information. As the mysterious agendas of mentally corrupt people begin to be seen in powerful positions, the chance of mind control decreases gradually.

Made in the USA
Coppell, TX
15 April 2021